D1132582

PROJECT
TYRANNUS

A BLUEPRINT FOR BUILDING A
POWERFUL CAMPUS MINISTRY

MIKE PATTERSON

Cover Design: Jake Studer

For permission requests, questions, or input, please contact the author directly:

Dr. Mike Patterson: Mike.Patterson@usd21.org

SOPI Executive Editor—Chris Adams

SOPI Associate Editor—Dr. Jennifer Watkins

Interior Design: Adina Cucicov

ISBN: 9798354720644

Dedication

This book is dedicated to my father in the faith, Dr. Matt Sullivan. I am forever indebted to him for his sacrifice and investment to give me my first full-time ministry opportunity. Much of my godly character has been forged by Matt's gracious discipling. Not only did he officiate Chenelle's and my wedding, but he also appointed me as an Evangelist and Chenelle as a Women's Ministry Leader in God's Kingdom. This book is a product of his compassionate mentorship.

Acknowledgments

I FIRST AND FOREMOST want to thank Jesus Christ, who has always been my hero since my baptism at 13 years old on December 13, 1998. The guidance, mercy, and abundant love that He has continually poured out on me are undeserved. Anything good from this book is because of Jesus Christ.

Words cannot express how grateful I am for my beautiful wife, Chenelle. She has been my partner in the gospel in this incredible journey of life and has given me the most beautiful daughter, Bellamy. Her encouragement in this endeavor to write this book and her lifelong friendship mean everything to me.

I want to thank three men who have formed and shaped my walk with God because of their mentorship. The first is Dr. Matt Sullivan, to whom this book is dedicated. Matt taught me how to be a man of integrity and a godly husband. The second is Luke Speckman—the big brother I never had and my fellow dreamer as we evangelized the Northeast United States before the Spirit sent him to lead the South Asian Churches. Finally, Dr. Kip McKean ignited in me a fire to evangelize the nations in this generation. He is my favorite preacher. His vision, grace, and truth have given so many of us in the SoldOut Movement Family a flesh and blood example of Jesus Christ in the

21st century. Thank you, Kip, for allowing me to personally interview you so that particularly the first chapter on "The History of Campus Ministry" is enhanced by your eyewitness account.

In addition to the men listed above, I also want to thank two of the campus ministry heroes in the Movement, Dr. Raul Moreno and Marcel Turner, who have built model campus ministries in São Paulo, Brazil and Miami, Florida respectively. We have served in the same churches at various times; I have learned so much from them up close and from afar.

Lastly, this book would not be a reality without the sacrifices of those who poured in hours of editing, formatting, and constructive input for this book: Lisa Franko, Dr. Raul Moreno, Luke Speckman, Chenelle Patterson, Jake Studer, and the Boston International Christian Church Interns.

Many more could be mentioned. I am so thankful for all of you in God's Kingdom and pray this book is a way to reciprocate the treasures you have given me.

Dr. Mike Patterson
Boston, Massachusetts, USA
August 12, 2022

CONTENTS

FOREWORD

GOD DEEPLY LOVES His creation! He cherishes it so much that He sent His only begotten son, Jesus Christ, to die for humanity! God has longed throughout all time for the whole world to know Him. As the Apostle Paul stated with conviction, *"This is good, and pleases God our Savior, who wants all people to be saved and to come to a knowledge of the truth."* **(1 Timothy 2:3-4)**

The question then becomes: How is this monumental task accomplished for the world to know Jesus? The answer to this question is both simple and complex at the same time. It is done through the preaching of the gospel of Jesus. That said, spiritual, motivated, talented, and skillful leaders are needed to propagate the good news across the globe. These men and women are not easy to find. The need is great, and time is short! Multitudes must be inspired and filled with an all-consuming passion for accomplishing this most important of tasks. Paul urged his young protégé, Timothy, *"And the things you have heard me say in the presence of many witnesses entrust to reliable people who will also be qualified to teach others."* **(2 Timothy 2:2)**

Where do we find these precious *"reliable"* individuals? Though powerful leaders can be found everywhere, the largest concentration of them can be found on university campuses all around the world.

The universities are where many go to be trained, expecting to do something significant with their lives. Thus, the campus ministry needs to be the primary source of leadership on which we focus to propagate the gospel globally. Campus ministry is where Mike Patterson excels! Mike is one of the most effective and fruitful campus ministers in our fellowship. God has blessed him with very successful campus ministries at Arizona State University, Cal State University Long Beach, University of Central Florida, University of Florida, Boston University, Columbia University, Northeastern University, and even Harvard University!

Mike is a personal friend and confidant but also a very influential evangelist, who is now leading the International Christian Church in Boston, one of the world's premier campus cities. I love to hear Mike preach, as he is gifted with a generous dose of passion! God has used that contagious zeal to ignite the faith of many to enter the full-time ministry and become world conquerors as well!

In this timely and much-needed book, *Project Tyrannus*, Mike will grace us with his knowledge of over 20 years in the faith with loads of campus ministry principles and practicals. If you are just starting to lead a campus ministry, this is the book for you! If you have led campus ministries for many years, this is the book for you from an expert in the field! I have learned much about campus ministry from this great book! Get ready to be inspired, be willing to be instructed, and prepare for a "campus ministry revolution" that will raise up the future leaders who will turn this world upside-down for Jesus Christ!

Dr. Raul Moreno
Mexico City, Mexico
March 18, 2022

INTRODUCTION

DO YOU SEE THE NEED? Martin Luther King Jr., Mahatma Gandhi, Abraham Lincoln, Dr. Marie Curie, Mother Theresa, and Nelson Mandela: What do all these individuals have in common? They changed the world! They had a vision of something greater than themselves and were willing to pay the price to see it accomplished. At the top of the list should be Jesus Christ, who, without picking up a weapon or writing a document, began a revolution that changed the world. As a Rabbi, Jesus "tapped into" the university system of His day. If you want to imitate this world-changer, campus ministry is the place to do it. Jesus Christ is the only way for a young person to make an eternal mark in this world!

The evangelization of the nations in our generation is dependent on the campus ministry. That may seem like a bold statement at first glance, but it is clear even to the world that tomorrow's future leaders reside on college campuses. The campus ministry is the center stage for the world's future politicians, CEOs, doctors, lawyers, scientists, professors, and entrepreneurs. In many cases, it is also the most internationally diverse setting of any city. My first job as a campus minister was at Arizona State University (ASU), at the time the nation's largest four-year university, boasting over 60,000 students. I came to realize that with the international diversity at ASU, the planet could be evangelized from that one college alone!

As of this writing, I currently serve the Lord as the Boston International Christian Church Evangelist. Through the years, it has been an honor to minister at such prestigious colleges as Harvard University, Columbia University, and Massachusetts Institute of Technology (MIT), fountains of leadership for the world and even more so for God's kingdom. For example, the daughter of former President Obama was invited to a Bible study by one of the disciples at Harvard! The opportunity for global impact is limitless on campus. Most incoming students are trying to figure out how they will make their mark in this world, but as disciples, we know that there is no other way to make a real impact except through Jesus Christ!

It is on the campuses that we find idealistic young people. They are unencumbered with "life's baggage," which makes mentoring them as "blank slates" highly effective. Ultimately, since they are young, your congregation becomes blessed with an infusion of vitality and energy as they train and lead.

Project Tyrannus is written as a practical guidebook. Surprisingly, there are very few books on the "How-tos" of building a thriving campus ministry. This book is for the evangelist wanting to start a campus ministry in his church; the discouraged campus minister feeling stuck with no results; the newly baptized disciple wanting to impact his campus for Christ; the single professional, single parent, or the married couple desiring to understand why campus ministry is the lifeblood of the church. This book is for any and everyone who truly wants to change the world!

Today truth has become subjective, and many students are confused about what their purpose for living is. Depression has swept the globe as economies fail, heroes and role models fail, and many families fail. Many are graduating from colleges and universities finding that their degrees barely help them gain employment, let alone attain the life of which they dreamed. School shootings are at an all-time high, and atheism is on the rise. Homosexuality is now not only widely accepted in many societies but also embraced and defended by the media. The Bible is considered, at best, good fictional literature, and at worst, a tool for "fundamental conservatives" to "control people." The "Christian groups" on campus are predominantly filled with students who grew up in their respective denominations with few personal convictions or none at all. Most "Christian" denominational statistics will show that their campus groups are declining at an alarming rate as our society becomes more "post-Christian."[1] The decline in church attendance means that in the upcoming years their ·influence will wane even more. There are pagan, gay, and occult clubs on campus that are consistently promoted and encouraged yet starting a "Christian club" has become increasingly challenging in my experience. Many have become discouraged and feel that the college field is no longer open to the gospel. Even among true disciples of Jesus, there can be a general feeling that we will convert a only few students, and our impact on today's fast-changing culture will be minimal at best.

This book proposes to crush this lie from Satan and show that students are more open to the gospel than ever and indeed are desperately

---

1   "Post-Christian" is a common term used to define a time in which Christianity is no longer the dominant religion or worldview of a society.

crying out for answers. Through biblical principles applied with simple techniques, we will see scores of campus students won for God. Revolution is brewing in the hearts of young men and women in colleges all around the world. We see their passion in recent politics and the current racial and social movements in our country, such as "Black Lives Matter" and the "LGBTQ+ Movement." Students still desire to change this world! A recent article from *USA Today* summarizes relevant statistics from a 2016 study done by UCLA:

> *According to a long-running annual UCLA study published in 2016, college students are more likely than ever to be involved in political and civic engagement. The study found one in 10 students expected to be involved in some kind of protest during their college career—the highest the survey had recorded since it began in 1967.*[2]

The highest since 1967? That was the year the Mainline Churches of Christ initiated campus ministry on the secular campuses, and it seems we are ready for another revival! It is time for us to change our perspective on the current trends on our campuses. "Acceptance" and "tolerance" need to become positive words for us as Christians because this means that students will now be more "open-minded" and accepting of the truth! The perversion we see on our campuses is a cry out for the love that only God can give. Atheism needs to be seen through the eyes of compassion as a symptom of many who have been deeply wounded by religion. It is an opportunity allowed by God for us as disciples to grow in using logic to show that belief in God is reasonable.

---

2   Casey Smith, "Is this the Golden Age of College Student Activism?" *USA Today College*, March 23rd, 2017.

God's ability to initiate a revolution in our colleges is dependent on His people's faith. As Jesus is amazed at the lack of faith surrounding his hometown ministry **(Mark 6:1-6)**, God must feel the same way as so few souls are saved on today's campuses because of our lack of faith! What if we changed our perspective to see the hunger and thirst for God that is being expressed in ungodly ways that usually repel us? Look at the hearts of college students today. They are "pro-love," "anti-bullying," and more focused on protecting the environment than ever! Without question, there is a desire to impact the world. We must show this hurting generation that Jesus Christ is the way to change the world—one person at a time! Jesus looked at the prostitutes and tax collectors with eyes full of love. We also need to see past the illusions of atheism, past the smokescreens of acceptance and tolerance of relative truth, and past the various types of confused sexuality in our society. Behind these shadows lies the reality of lost souls "looking for love in all the wrong places."

Students are just as passionate about changing the world now as ever.

The "blueprint" for building a powerful campus ministry is the Word of God. *Project Tyrannus* will take a detailed look at the campus ministry initiated by Paul in Ephesus around AD 54 in Acts 19:8-10, where he imitated the ministry principles of Jesus and His Apostles. This passage will serve as the outline for this book, a blueprint if you will, on which you can model your campus ministry and expect the same results as the Apostle Paul. Each chapter takes a portion of Acts 19:8-10 to glean insights into how Paul built a campus ministry that changed the world. Prayerfully, *Project Tyrannus* will soften our hearts so we can once again embrace Jesus' vision that the *"fields are ripe for harvest"*—especially on college campuses. **(John 4:35)** And to God be the glory!

CHAPTER 1

THE HISTORY OF
CAMPUS MINISTRY

"For everything that was written in the past was written to teach us, so that through the endurance taught in the Scriptures and the encouragement they provide we might have hope."

– ROMANS 15:4

A PROFOUND TRUTH: "Those who do not learn history are doomed to repeat it." (George Santayana) However, those who do, build even better! Working with campus-aged men and women was one of the secrets of Jesus' ministry, which led to the spread of Christianity all over the world in that generation. However, for centuries after the Apostles and their disciples passed away, the world was une-vangelized with the true gospel. Tapping into the understanding of changing the world through young people, Bill Bright's Campus Crusade (CRU) showed, by the early 1950s with their success at

UCLA, that it was possible to bring a message about Jesus Christ to secular colleges; though it must be noted that they did not teach the full truth about salvation.

In 1967, the Mainline Churches of Christ (MCOC)—inspired by Campus Crusade—pioneered an evangelistic secular campus ministry at the 14th Street Church of Christ with a vision to reach out to the University of Florida. This new effort was called "Campus Advance" and was led by Chuck Lucas. From this seed came what was known as the "Crossroads Movement." By 1979, the Spirit initiated the Boston Movement in Lexington, Massachusetts, with a small group of "30 would-be disciples." This movement was propelled by campus converts from the Crossroads Movement and from other MCOC Campus Movements around America. The Boston Movement leader, Kip McKean, was baptized at the University of Florida in 1972. Having campus ministry as the primary focus was one of the key factors for the Boston movement becoming the fastest growing "Christian Movement" in the world in the 1980s and 1990s. By 1994, the Boston Movement officially became known as the International Churches of Christ (ICOC). Tragically, Satan demolished this heroic effort in the early 2000s.

Yet in 2006, the Spirit initiated the SoldOut Discipling Movement— the International Christian Churches—from the Portland, Oregon ICOC. Learning from the past efforts of the MCOC and the ICOC, Kip led this radical congregation, raising up many young leaders and thus advancing the "New Movement." God used him to gather and multiply a remnant that became a powerful family of churches whose focus—as in the ICOC—was campus ministry. One of the great innovations in the New Movement was the founding of the

International College of Christian Ministries (ICCM) in 2012, which augmented the one-on-one mentoring of future Evangelists and Women's Ministry Leaders with in-depth biblical instruction. So, some 47 years after Campus Advance was initiated, I was honored in 2014 to become the University of Florida Campus Minister in this new global SoldOut Movement.

In that day the remnant of Israel, the survivors of Jacob, will no longer rely on him who struck them down but will truly rely on the LORD, the Holy One of Israel. A remnant will return, a remnant of Jacob will return to the Mighty God.

-ISAIAH 10:20-21

In the aforementioned passage, God's judgment on Israel for their disobedience would come through the Assyrian army. Yet, God promised that He would leave a remnant (literally "survivors") that would come together again and return to Him. Throughout the Scriptures, God has always called out a remnant that has committed themselves to His work: Noah and his family, Jacob and his twelve sons, Gideon and the 300, David and his mighty men, Zerubbabel and the exiles who returned from Babylon to Jerusalem to rebuild God's Temple, and the Jews who became the first Christians. Jesus said, *"Whoever is not with me is against me, and whoever does not gather with me scatters."* **(Luke 11:23)** Jesus' work was to gather disciples into a brotherhood to see the world evangelized. It is the will of God for *"...all men to be saved and to come to a knowledge of the truth."* **(1 Timothy 2:4)** Only a unified global church with an emphasis on campus ministry can accomplish the evangelization of the nations in our generation. You cannot reach the whole world in a generation without reaching its youth.

Education has always been integral to Christendom. From the beginning, Jesus was the Rabbi of the *"unschooled and ordinary"* Apostles. **(Acts 4:13)** Interestingly, the European Degree System from which the Bachelor's, Master's, and Doctorate Degrees originate is rooted in the development of the church. In the early church, the Apostles and other Christian leaders were called "doctors." Later, in the Middle Ages, the Doctorate Degree was awarded to someone who was accredited to teach in a university. Given the church's apostasy and the combining of "church and state," this "campus ministry" was certainly not one that would change the world. Still, even colleges in the past few centuries were founded to produce "Christian" leadership. Many of the Ivy League Colleges in America were established to train preachers—Harvard University in 1636 and Yale University in 1702 being two examples.

In England, one of the first campus ministries initiated after the Middle Ages was Oxford University's "Holy Clubs." John and Charles Wesley gathered small groups composed of Oxford students who pursued holiness and met for Bible study and prayer. George Whitefield was raised up from this effort at Oxford. Upon graduation, Whitefield traveled with the Wesley Brothers to North America and became a key figure in the "First Great Awakening" which spanned from 1730-1770.

Later, in the United States, students began gathering for prayer times on campus. One of the earliest examples comes from 1787 at the beginning of the "Second Great Awakening," as five students in a dormitory room at Hampden Sydney College in Virginia gathered for prayer. The student body was "deists at best and atheists at worst."³ R. Rowland quoted Bill Bright in the following account of this epic event:

Five ordinary students—not even Christians—had finally become disgusted with the blatantly immoral climate on their campus. As a last resort, they decided to hold a prayer meeting to ask for God's help. Fearing the reaction of other students, they locked themselves in a room and kept their voices down so they would not be found out.

However, other students discovered them and tried to break down the door. The president of the college [John Blair Smith] heard the disturbance and came to find out who had started the latest riot. One of the students outside said, "Oh, sir, it's nothing important; there are just some fanatics in here holding a prayer meeting! Can you imagine? So we thought we'd teach them a lesson. We won't hurt them. We'll rough them up a little bit, but we won't hurt them."

The president rebuked them saying, "You don't mind cheating, you don't mind stealing from rooms, you don't mind the lying and the profanity you get on this campus, but you object to a prayer meeting. Well, I do not!" He then knocked on the door and said authoritatively, "This is the president of the college speaking. Will you please come out?" The students unlocked the door

---

3   "Reflection—Prayer at Hampden-Sydney College," Hearts for the Lost, accessed September 7, 2022, https://heartsforthelost.com/posts/biblical-revival-a-historical-reflection-prayer-at-hampden-sydney-college/.

and came out, not knowing what to expect. President Smith said, "Gentlemen, come to my study; we'll pray there together."[4]

In 1886, the Student Volunteer Movement for Foreign Missions was founded in America directly appealing to college students for their membership.

[The Student Volunteer Movement] originated at a conference held in July 1886 at Mt. Hermon, Massachusetts. The conference, called by the Young Men's Christian Association [YMCA] with the Protestant evangelist Dwight Lyman Moody as the leader, was attended by 251 men from 89 colleges and universities in the United States and Canada. When the conference closed, 100 of the group led by Robert P. Wilder of Princeton University, had decided to become foreign missionaries. In the ensuing year, Wilder... toured colleges, universities, and theological seminaries, seeking to enlist others. An organization was formed with John Raleigh Mott, who had been at Mt. Hermon, as Chairman of the Executive Committee. For 33 years, Mott directed the movement. Students became members of the movement by signing the declaration: "It is my purpose, if God permits, to become a foreign missionary." Their watch-word, "the evangelization of the world in this generation," expressed their belief that all Christians had the duty of making the gospel known to their contemporaries throughout the world. Student Volunteer "Bands" were organized at many colleges, universities, and theological seminaries throughout the United States. Wilder carried the message also

---

4   R. Rowland. *Campus Ministries: A Historical Study of Churches of Christ Campus Ministries and Select College Ministries from 1706 to 1990.* (Star Bible Publications, 1991), 7.

to the British Isles and Europe, and similar movements arose in several countries.[5]

So important to understand, in light of Kip McKean forming a central leadership in the ICOC and ICC, is that the Student Volunteer Movement strove to accomplish its noble task with a central leadership, yet sadly taught a false doctrine for salvation.

Around the same time in the 1890s, many American denominational campus ministries transitioned into what is known as "Bible Chairs." A Bible Chair was a "teaching chair" (head of an academic department) with which a denomination was given the opportunity by the college to open a new department to teach the Bible, most often for college credit. The goal would be to convert the students who would take these Bible courses. Often the denomination would build a facility where students were taught and enjoyed recreational activities and meals together. Over the next ninety years or so, the impact of the "Bible Chair Method" greatly lessened because of the secularization of college faculties, the "pushback" by many humanistic groups, and the overall disinterest of the student body in the Bible.

The Mainline Church of Christ (MCOC) was birthed out of the Restoration Movement of the early 1800s. The movement was revolutionary in restoring God's plan of salvation to repent and be baptized for the forgiveness of sins. **(Acts 2:38)** Alexander Campbell, who is regarded as one of the founders of the MCOC, interestingly

---

5 "Student Volunteer Movement," Encyclopedia.com, accessed September 4, 2022, https://www.encyclopedia.com/religion/encyclopedias-almanacs-transcripts-and-maps/student-volunteer-movement.

was not baptized with the understanding that it was for the forgiveness of sins, but was baptized as an adult by full immersion in water as he saw it to be the command of God. Years later, he began to teach that baptism was in fact the point where sin was forgiven. The result was that many Baptists "joined"—placed membership—in the MCOC with this same false thinking, retroactively looking back at their baptisms as being done for forgiveness. This is counter to the biblical teaching that one must go into the water understanding their sins are being forgiven. (John 3:5; Acts 2:38)

During the late 1800s and 1900s, most young people in America in the MCOC attended newly founded "Christian Colleges." Among these colleges are Lipscomb University (1891), Abilene Christian University (1906), Harding University (1924), Pepperdine University (1937), and Oklahoma Christian University (1950), which I attended. The predominant thinking was for parents to send their children to MCOC Colleges to be "protected" from the world and find Christian spouses. The very zealous young people who wanted to go into the full-time ministry sometimes chose to go to "Schools of Preaching," such as the Sunset School of Preaching and the Preston Road School of Preaching. However, a growing number of MCOC youth wanted to attend secular colleges. Most fell away unless they were involved in a Bible Chair.

Seeing this phenomenon, five separate campus ministry movements would evolve in the MCOC in the 1960s and 1970s and were spearheaded by Stephen D. Eckstein (Portales, New Mexico), Stanley Shipp assisted by Ryan Howard (St. Louis, Missouri), Dr. John Wilson assisted by Tom Jones, (Springfield, Missouri), Milton Jones (Seattle, Washington), and Charles (Chuck) Lucas assisted by Sam

Laing (Gainesville, Florida). Though all these movements were in the MCOC, they were not unified.

Steve Eckstein played an important role in advancing the MCOC Campus Ministries since he personally graduated from Eastern New Mexico University's Bible Chair. He eventually became the Bible Chair Director at his alma mater, where he stayed for 33 years. Though many argued that academics and evangelism could not go hand in hand, Eckstein led many students to Christ using this scholarly approach. In the 1960s, most MCOC Leaders considered the Bible Chair Method as the most effective in reaching out to secular college students. In time, Eckstein would begin what became known as the National Campus Ministers Seminar by contacting all the Bible Chairs in America that he knew about to attend these national meetings. Later, he would invite the leaders from the other MCOC Campus Ministry Movements. Kip admired Steve Eckstein's bold vision, and Kip complimented him in his writings. However, though edifying to Christians, the MCOC approach to having a "campus ministry conference" did not create true unity.

Of note, participants of the National Campus Ministers Seminar (NCMS) on the last day would vote for the host of the next year's NCMS. Amazingly, after Kip had been in Boston for only one year, the Boston Church (then the Lexington Church of Christ) had baptized so many students that it was voted to be the host of the 1981 NCMS. At the 1981 NCMS Banquet, Chuck Lucas confided to Kip that his biggest mistake in building the Crossroads Church was not having a discipling relationship with the elders. To the end of Chuck's leadership tenure at Crossroads, the elders were the ultimate leaders of this autonomous congregation. In 1988 when

Kip selected "World Sector Leaders," thus forming a formal central leadership, most of the MCOC Churches disfellowshipped him and the Boston Churches. Consequently, the Boston Movement members stopped attending the NCMS.

Stanley Shipp, who had a major influence on the campus ministries and the Mainline Churches of Christ in the St. Louis Area, called for the evangelization of secular students. They had small group discussions to this effect. Shipp was controversial, as some believed he was accepting of the existence of charismatic gifts in the church, as well as having women lead prayers. Interestingly, his associate Ryan Howard was "re-baptized" in the Boston Movement in the 1980s.

Dr. John Wilson, a Southwest Missouri State University Religion Professor and MCOC Campus Minister, believed the Bible Chairs and student centers of the MCOC served to build a fence around its students, protecting them from worldly influence.[6] Yet he was progressive in wanting a direct outreach on campus. Sadly, Wilson strongly opposed Chuck Lucas and the Crossroads Movement as he felt they possessed an arrogant attitude because of their "greater success" and "exercised control through one-on-one discipling" that was "unchristian." To their credit, Wilson, along with Tom Jones, trained campus ministers and sent them out from Springfield, Missouri. Of note was Greg Jackson, who started the campus ministry at Indiana State University whose first convert was John Causey. Later, Tom Jones was "re-baptized" in the Boston Movement in the 1980s which influenced John and Emma Causey to join as well.

---

6   John F. Wilson, "Campus Ministry Perspective on the World" (Lecture, National Campus Ministers' Seminar, Search, AR, August 8, 1978).

Another campus movement of the 1970s was led by Milton Jones, a campus minister who began his work at the University of Washington and who later wrote *Discipling: The Multiplying Ministry*. Milton's campus ministry was supported by the Northwest Church of Christ; there was a heavy focus on evangelism, and his influence spanned throughout the Northwest USA. Eckstein's first National Campus Ministers Seminar in 1957 only had a few campus ministers present, but the seminar in 1982, directed by Milton Jones, saw over 250 attend in Seattle, Washington. Crossroads supporters questioned Milton Jones because of the evening speaker selection. Jones had asked Don Williams, a Pepperdine University Bible Professor, to speak. Those in the Crossroads Movement felt that he had not baptized enough students to be qualified to speak. Interestingly, later Kip asked Milton and his wife to come to Boston for further training. He declined. We see among these campus ministry movements divisions in philosophy, thought, and even doctrine.[7]

In 1967, Chuck Lucas was hired by the elders of the 14th Street Church of Christ to be the campus minister and begin an "experimental" program to reach out to University of Florida students. Three years later, he became the pulpit minister, and Sam Laing was hired to be the campus minister. In 1973, after moving to a new building, the 14th Street Church of Christ was renamed the Crossroads Church of Christ. Since they baptized and trained campus ministers and sent them into existing churches, those churches became known as the "Crossroads Movement"—also called the "Total Commitment Movement." The motivating vision of the Crossroads Movement was

---

7   John F. Wilson, "History of Campus Ministries in the Churches of Christ" (Lecture for Religion 592 class, Campus Ministry Organizational and Administration, Pepperdine University, Malibu, CA, fall 1983).

to initiate and build a thriving campus ministry on every college in the United States. Well documented at that time was that the average MCOC congregation was 150 members, yet had only eight baptisms per year. Six of the baptisms were children of the members of the church. Over 90% of the other baptisms from the world would fall away. Many considered the MCOC dead or at best lukewarm, and so the number of campus converts from the Crossroads Campus Ministries was in stark contrast. The Crossroads Church—as with all the churches to which they sent campus ministers—had a large number of uncommitted adult members. For example, many of the adult members did not come to a midweek service, a few even went outside after Sunday service and smoked cigarettes. This group wanted no part of discipleship. Disunity came not only into the Crossroads Church, but also into the MCOC congregations to which they had sent their young ministers. The college students they converted would be fired up, but the older members remained lukewarm, resulting in conflict.

In 1967, Lucas started with 10 Mainline Church of Christ students. According to Rowland's book *Campus Ministries: A Historical Study*, in 1968, 35 people were baptized at the 14th Street Church of Christ, with a church membership of around 100. A paragraph from the booklet entitled "Crossroads Church of Christ History and Highlights" shows us what happened next:

In 1970, the congregation averaged 218 in Sunday morning services and immersed 81 during the year. In 1971, there were 109 baptized and a total of 375 responses. In 1973, the average Sunday attendance was 300 while 27 Soul Talks took place on the campus of the University of Florida (14 for the men and 12 for the women) along with 13 other non-campus Soul Talks. (Soul Talks were small group Bible studies, whose purpose was to reach out to non-Christians.) 1974 statistics show 500 members, with 70 placing membership during the year, along with 237 baptisms which were the highest reported in any one year at Crossroads. ... From the start of the Campus Advance work in 1967 until 1974, 895 baptisms were recorded by the congregation... Crossroads reached its highest membership in 1978 with 1,019.[8]

The "Crossroads Church of Christ" would pack the building with college students who wanted to make an impact for Christ!

To be clear, from the historical record the highest number of baptisms ever recorded at the Crossroads Church was in 1974 with 237 baptisms. Also, the membership peaked in 1978 at 1,019. Except for the Boston Church, no "Crossroads Campus Ministry Church" ever

---

8   Rowland, *Campus Ministries*, 95.

baptized 237 people in a year or had a membership over 1,000. These statistics represent the slow decline of the Crossroads Movement and the need for a more radical approach to church-building which would allow the continued multiplication of baptisms and campus ministries.

Kip McKean was baptized through the efforts of the 14th Street Church of Christ as a 17-year-old, University of Florida freshman on April 11, 1972. After a year, he gave up his pre-med studies and trained for the campus ministry at the Crossroads Church under Chuck Lucas and Sam Laing. In 1975, Kip's first full-time ministry assignment was to be the "campus minister" at the MCOC College—Northeastern Christian College (NCC)—just outside of Philadelphia, Pennsylvania. During this difficult year, Kip's focus shifted from working at NCC to reaching out to the secular campuses of Haverford, Bryn Mawr, and Villanova. Though he had a slow start that even made him question staying in the ministry, in his last 18 weeks with the King of Prussia Church of Christ, God blessed him with 18 baptisms. Since the preacher and three of the six elders at the King of Prussia Church of Christ did not believe one had to be baptized to be saved, it was obvious to Kip that he had to move on.

Kip then became the Campus Minister for the 100-member Heritage Chapel Church in the small town of Charleston, Illinois. In only three years, Kip and his newlywed wife Elena saw 300 Eastern Illinois University students baptized into Christ. During this time, many observed that churches that had Crossroads-trained ministers often split. The commitment of the campus ministry "shined a light" on the lukewarmness of the adults. Kip came to the biblical conviction that not only should college students be called to total commitment, but the adults as well. Kip came to the conviction from Jesus' teaching that *"no one puts new wine into old wineskins. If he does, the new wine will burst the skins and it will be spilled, and the skins will be destroyed but new wine must be put into new wineskins."* **(Luke 5:37-38)** He would recognize that the Crossroad's minister (new wine) would go into a lukewarm church (old wineskin), and both the minister and the church would be ruined. The campus minister would usually be discouraged, and sometimes the church would split. The thriving campus ministries would then see their growth capped at some point if they continued to exist in a lukewarm church as—so to speak—"a church within a church." Influenced by the Scriptures and principles illuminated in such books as Robert Coleman's *Master Plan of Evangelism,* the Spirit clarified to Kip that the key was to build churches in which every member was totally committed and to plant churches through mission teams composed of only sold-out disciples. Kip has continued to preach to this day that new sold-out ministers must go into new sold-out churches.[9]

So, summarizing, these five campus movements had some impact, yet they did not work together, ultimately being limited in influence by autonomy and lukewarmness. With so much division, how could the campus ministries truly impact America, let alone the world? The Crossroads Movement, though revolutionary in its call for total commitment and evangelism for campus students, refused to take a stand against the lukewarmness and false doctrines of the

---

9   "Sold-out" is a term based on **Matthew 13:44-45** where someone who is a disciple is willing to give up everything to be totally committed. The ICC is known as the "SoldOut Movement." A sold-out disciple is the only type of disciple there is biblically.

MCOC. However, Kip would be contacted by a small church of 60 in Lexington, Massachusetts, where he was interviewed to be the pulpit minister and campus minister. If they were to be hired, Kip and his wife Elena made it clear that every member would be called to be totally committed. On Friday, June 1st of 1979, Kip arrived in Boston, and on that first night in the home of Bob and Pat Gempel, he called the "30 would-be disciples" to total commitment.

At this point, the Lexington Church (soon to become the Boston Church of Christ) was still viewed as a Crossroads Campus Ministry Church. The following differences would soon become obvious: The revolutionary call for *every member* (campus, single, married, and teen) to be "totally committed;" the call for every member to be in a "one-on-one discipling relationship;" the vision to evangelize the nations in one generation; and the eventual stand against the unbiblical doctrine of autonomy, which spurred Kip on to creating a central leadership. (See Appendix I and Ron Harding's *The Untold Story: Chronicles of Modern-Day Christianity.*) In 10 years, the Boston Church of Christ would grow to 4,000 on Sundays while meeting in the famed Boston Garden. Unprecedented in modern times, the Boston Church had over 1,000 campus disciples by 1989! This becomes all the more amazing since the students attended such prestigious colleges as Harvard and MIT. The growth was unheard of in New England, which had always been viewed as a mission field by the MCOC. The Boston Church of Christ was the largest church of *any* kind in the history of New England and the largest congregation in the MCOC in the entire world!

In 1985, when Chuck Lucas resigned from the ministry for personal reasons, God placed on Kip's heart a desire to unify the Crossroads

Campus Ministry Churches with the Boston Movement. As well, Kip wanted to unify all the campus ministry movements into one movement. He found that relatively few from the other movements had the heart to be totally committed. The exception was the Crossroad Campus Ministry Churches. Half of these churches invited Kip and the Boston Movement to call every member of their congregation to total commitment in one weekend. This process was called "reconstruction." After the reconstruction, only one-fifth to one-third would remain, but these churches were filled with only totally committed members. The most notable reconstructions were Kingston, Jamaica; San Francisco, California; Atlanta, Georgia; Orlando, Florida; and San Diego, California. Thus, there was no difference between Boston plantings and the reconstructions.

From 1982-1988, Kip estimates that 3,000-4,000 college students or graduates moved to Boston or its plantings or became members of reconstructed churches. This greatly accelerated the planting of churches around the world. Also key to multiplying congregations, Kip came to convictions contrary to the Mainline Church of Christ concerning how one views the Bible. The MCOC does believe that the Old Testament and New Testament are inspired by God, but only the New Testament can be used in church governance. From 2 Timothy 3:16-17, Kip believed that we are to be a "Bible Church" and not simply a "New Testament Church" as Paul taught *"all Scripture is from God."* The word *"Scripture"* in the New Testament only refers to what we call the Old Testament. (Of course, the Law of the Old Testament is no longer binding.) Also, Kip rejected the MCOC theology from Thomas Campbell that "we are to speak where the Bible speaks and be silent where the Bible is silent." Kip believed that "we are to be silent where the Bible speaks and speak where the Bible is silent." In other words, if the Bible teaches something, we are to obey; yet, where it is silent, we have the freedom to come up with methods to carry out God's commands. In 1987, Crossroads—clinging to the MCOC mode of Biblical interpretation—opposed Kip and the Boston Movement and formally disfellowshipped them.

The Boston Movement became known as the International Churches of Christ in 1994 as it was planting churches worldwide. As well in 1994, Kip penned the "Evangelization Proclamation," whose vision was to plant a church in every nation that had a city of at least 100,000 in population. This momentous task was completed in the year 2000! Some wrongly thought that the Boston Movement was not focusing on or was drifting away from campus ministry by emphasizing that every member (married, single, campus, and teen) needed to be fully committed. Nothing could be further from the truth! These three convictions that the world needs to be evangelized in one generation, that the movement needs a central leader and central leadership, and that the church needs to be composed of only sold-out disciples ("totally committed" was the previous terminology) are the convictions that allowed campus ministry to explode not only in Boston, not only in America but all around the world! Boston and the plantings of Moscow, Manila, and Los Angeles had campus ministries of well over 1,000 students.

The vision of the world being evangelized was the command given in the great commission by Jesus Christ. (**Matthew 28:18-20**) In the MCOC, the purpose was understood to win souls, but the overarching vision of world evangelism was foreign to many. This motivating vision gave the ICOC even more of a reason to be on college campuses. International students could become Christians and then, upon graduation, be called to "go home" to help with church plantings in their homelands. Nationals from college ministry provided a fountain of leadership to get *"to the ends of the earth."* (**Acts 1:8**) College students throughout history have always desired to be a part of something larger than themselves. Without this core conviction to see the world won, college ministries wane and the graduating students tend to become lukewarm.

To reiterate, the Mainline Churches of Christ could never mobilize their college students to work together. Earlier we saw five different campus movements from the 1970s which were never unified; though they had great campus seminars and hot pockets of fired-up college students for Christ, no one could work together to send these students on mission teams or share money and resources to accomplish the task of winning the world. The ICOC with a central leadership could now grow its campus ministries rapidly by building a global brotherhood. If a campus ministry or church was hurting, it could send in help; if a church needed to be planted, it could call upon members from different congregations to help meet the need. College students in the congregations could also find Christian spouses in any city where a church was planted without worrying about varying degrees of commitment and conflicting biblical convictions.

The conviction that the church is composed of only sold-out disciples prevented in-fighting and a tolerance of "different levels of commitment." While leading the church in Boston, Kip developed a Bible study series called *First Principles* that gave everyone a unified toolset to make disciples. One study was developed while Kip was doing campus ministry at Harvard. While helping someone see the difference between what the Boston Church taught and what their church taught, Kip explained from the Scriptures that a disciple and a Christian are the same (**Acts 11:25-26**), that to be baptized one must decide to be a disciple, and that one must have the heart to be discipled by another disciple. (**Matthew 28:19-20, John 4:1-2**) He went on to say that the true church was to be composed of only sold-out disciples. It is clear the ICOC did not get away from campus ministry; quite the opposite, its restored biblical doctrines allowed it to grow even more rapidly.

Sadly, in 2001, one of Kip's children began to struggle spiritually, and the ICOC leadership began to question whether the McKeans were fit to lead during this vulnerable time in their lives. First, a sabbatical was announced, and then a coup was orchestrated by those in the central leadership who shared a Mainline Church of Christ background and theology. At this point, the leadership of the ICOC Churches was taken away from the McKeans. In 2003, the McKeans were fired for the very same convictions that created the Boston Movement and built ICOC Churches around the world. The ICOC renounced biblical convictions, and through the efforts of the leadership with MCOC roots, they brought the church back to a more MCOC theology. As a result, thousands fell away, and lukewarmness ravaged the churches. The McKeans courageously took a stand to hold on to the core convictions that were the backbone of the church while acknowledging mistakes, but it became clear that *"no remedy"* was left for the ICOC. (**2 Chronicles 36:16**)

In 2003, the Spirit sent the McKeans to lead the Portland, Oregon ICOC. In January 2003, the church had 300 members but by the time the McKeans arrived just seven months later, they only had 25 members at Kip's first midweek service. Excitingly, the Spirit would revive this small church to become one of the few growing churches, in fact, the fastest growing church, in the ICOC all around the world. As the baptisms started coming again, disciples from 26 of the 50 States in America moved to Portland. The Portland Church would grow from those 25 to 487 members in only three years, with over 600 in attendance on Sundays.

In 2004, I had the opportunity to visit the Portland Church. As a result, I was moved to leave my lukewarm ICOC congregation and join what was becoming known as the "Portland Movement" within the ICOC, which eventually would be disfellowshipped from the ICOC and become the SoldOut Movement in 2006. I had been attending the Manhattan Christian College in Kansas when I visited Portland. After being inspired by the ministry of the Portland Church, I transferred to Cascade College—a branch of Oklahoma Christian College in Portland. I am so grateful for this experience because I did not understand why my campus ministry had died, and many of my friends had fallen away back at home. To me, it was obvious that they had become lukewarm, but later I understood that foundational convictions were also renounced—lukewarmness was the by-product. No central leadership had clearly communicated about this decision to return to MCOC theology, because part of this theology held each church to be autonomous, the very reason they had no central leadership in the first place!

I decided to move to Portland because I just wanted to be part of the church in which I was originally baptized, and this was the church I saw on my visit to Portland. Also, attending an MCOC

College helped me see that there was really no doctrinal difference between what became of the ICOC and the MCOC. Courageously, Kip continued to teach from the Scriptures that God's plan was: 1) Discipling was a command and not optional, 2) In the New Testament, the churches were not autonomous, and 3) Jesus and the Apostles had the vision to evangelize the nations in a generation, which the ICOC had labeled as "impossible."

The zealous Portland Campus Ministry was perhaps the most inspiring to me personally upon visiting. Portland's original 25 only had four college students and one teen. After three years of focus from Kip and Elena (then 49 and 48 years old respectively), they built a campus ministry of over 100 college students and almost 40 teens. So why were there so few campus ministries growing in the ICOC or the MCOC? The reason was the rejecting of those foundational doctrines needed to build and sustain a powerful campus ministry—the MCOC theology of autonomy was a death blow to most churches and therefore to their campus ministries.

The Spirit made it clear to Kip and many around the world that it was time to "start again" in the fall of 2006. So, God initiated the SoldOut Movement (International Christian Churches), which was formally announced in a three-part series in the Portland Church Bulletin entitled, "Partners in the Gospel." In 2007, the McKeans moved to Los Angeles to begin the City of Angels International Christian Church with a mission team of 42 Portland disciples, many of whom were converted through the campus and teen ministries. Amazingly, by August of 2022, God has multiplied this one congregation into over 10,000 disciples in 137 churches in 54 nations on every populated continent of the world. As we glance back at the history of Christendom, Kip stands on the broad shoulders of men of faith who took valiant stands for Jesus—yet did not teach the biblical plan of salvation of baptizing disciples for the remission of sins—such as Martin Luther, John and Charles Wesley, Dwight L. Moody, and Bill Bright. As well, without Restoration Movement pioneers—Alexander Campbell, Thomas Campbell, Barton Stone, Steve Eckstein, and Chuck Lucas—there would most likely not be Dr. Kip McKean, and yet in God's providence, He has raised Kip up in this generation.

If you are currently part of an autonomous congregation, the principles of this book might help you see *limited* success, but it most likely will not be sustainable. I would encourage you to dig deep into the Scriptures, reach out to disciples in the SoldOut Movement, and pray about making the same move I did.[10] Also, read other books that detail Kip's radical teachings, such as Ron Harding's *The Untold Story—Chronicles of Modern-Day Christianity,* Dr. Tim Kernan's *20/20 Books 1 & 2,* Dr. Jason Dimitry's *COPS—Company of Prophets*, and Dr. Elena McKean's *Elevate—Jesus' Global Revolution for Women.* Truth be told, there need to be many, many more dynamic campus ministries of sold-out disciples devoted to the proclamation of the gospel. Let us heed Paul's exhortation,

Now to Him who is able to establish you by my gospel and the proclamation of Jesus Christ, according to the revelation of the mystery hidden for long ages past, but now revealed and made known through the prophetic writings by

---

10 "SoldOut Discipling Movement," USD21.org, accessed September 4, 2022, https://usd21.org. This website will give you a directory of SoldOut Movement churches around the world.

the command of the eternal God, so that all nations might believe and obey Him—to the only wise God be glory forever through Jesus Christ! Amen.

-ROMANS 16:25-27 NIV 1984)

Thus, I invite you to enter *Project Tyrannus*!

CHAPTER 2

ENTER INTO
PROJECT TYRANNUS

BEFORE WE ENTER *Project Tyrannus,* "Paul's campus ministry," we must enroll in the first campus ministry in the Bible, that of Jesus! Many overlook that Jesus was a professor, or in His day, a rabbi. Rabbi Jesus chose a school of twelve students (interestingly, the word disciple means literally "student"). This class also included women. **(Luke 8:1-3)** We can deduce that all the Apostles except Peter were under the age of twenty since Peter was the only one who could pay the temple tax, which you had to be twenty or older to do. **(Matthew 17:24-27)** These unschooled, ordinary men **(Acts 4:13)** would enter the "campus ministry" of Jesus for three years and produce some of the best Koine Greek writings of all time, the New Testament. They would also become the most powerful of preachers, equipped with the sword of God's Holy Spirit! **(Ephesians 6:17)**

If God's Modern-day Movement is to imitate Jesus, we must all, from one perspective, become "campus" students in the "University of Jesus." Jesus believed in a "school of prophets" similar to the one found in **2 Kings 2:3-5,** where He could walk with and teach his students.[11] So, before we talk about evangelizing our colleges, we need to understand the incredible blessing it is to have in God's modern-day movement our own University of Jesus, the International College of Christian Ministries (ICCM).

August 16th, 2012 was a historic day for the SoldOut Movement of churches as the California Bureau of Private Postsecondary Education approved our college with the "Verification of Exempt Status," allowing the ICCM to grant Bachelor's, Master's, and Doctoral Degrees in Ministry according to the SoldOut Movement's biblical doctrines and convictions. I would encourage anyone seriously considering the call of full-time ministry, whether at a campus ministry or church leader level, to pray about being called into the ICCM.

**ICCM is the SoldOut Movement's modern-day
"school of prophets"**

---

11 For an in-depth study on raising up future leaders, please read Jason Dimitry, *COPS Company of Prophets: Church Builders Field Manual* (SOPI, 2022).

ICCM is not a replacement for how Jesus trained His ministers by walking with them and discipling them for a period. Denominational seminaries often lack a foundation of biblical truth as well as the training of practical application necessary to equip ministers. I attended Oklahoma Christian University (a Church of Christ College), where received a Bachelor's degree in Biblical Studies, and also studied Greek at New Orleans Theological Baptist Seminary. Since the ICCM, however, combines academic learning with practical training as Jesus did with His disciples, I learned much more about ministry from the ICCM program than I ever did from those universities. I believe this is because ICCM is not simply another seminary where "*knowledge puffs up.*" (**1 Corinthians 8:1**) There is no depth of biblical training and practical ministry in the seminaries of the world. This is why many are jokingly called "cemeteries;" the idea is you go in full of faith and come out dead spiritually. It would be an amusing idea if it were not the very reason we have dead atheistic "preachers" behind thousands of pulpits today. On the other hand, ICCM is raising up a generation of the world's best preachers for God.

I share about ICCM because Jesus understood that His students— men and women—needed to enroll in His university before going to the "campus of the world," as we will see in Paul's life in a moment. ICCM also helps augment our practical training with pertinent biblical knowledge and allows us to get travel visas for our missionaries to evangelize the nations in our generation.

Paul, having been trained by Jesus for three years in Arabia, (**Galatians 1:12-18**) knew the value of walking with young leaders. Thus, we now encounter the first campus ministry in the Bible after the church started on the day of Pentecost.

In this, our theme passage, Luke describes how Paul built a pillar church in Ephesus on the foundation of a campus ministry.

Paul entered the synagogue and spoke boldly there for three months, arguing persuasively about the Kingdom of God. But some of them became obstinate; they refused to believe and publicly maligned the Way. So Paul left them. He took the disciples with him and had discussions daily in the lecture hall of Tyrannus. This went on for two years, so that all the Jews and Greeks who lived in the province of Asia heard the Word of the Lord.

-ACTS 19:8-10

The Apostle Paul always had a strategy when it came to evangelism. As seen in Luke's account of the historic church in the Book of Acts, his worldwide strategy was to build churches in *leading cities* (**Acts 16:12**) that could evangelize the surrounding area. This approach is seen in his focus on getting to Rome, the leading city of the empire, (**Acts 19:21; 23:11**) as he begins to realize his destiny and call to bear witness to the Gentiles. Paul had been born a Roman citizen in Tarsus of Cilicia, and in his missionary journeys, he began to realize why God allowed him to be a citizen. He could use it to his advantage to have special rights, even to appeal to Caesar when being persecuted. (**Acts 25:9-12**) God used Paul's ethnicity, citizenship, education, and cultural background to evangelize the world in his generation!

The author is pictured in front of the Religious Life Office at Columbia University with his mentor Luke Speckman, who served as one of the Religious Life Advisors at that prestigious campus.

The fact that you were accepted into the college you were accepted into is because God has a divine purpose for you there, just as He had for Paul. (**Acts 17:26-28**) In the apostle's missionary journeys, we also see a local strategy Paul implemented to preach the gospel. He would first evangelize the Jews in the local synagogue and then when the Jews started to persecute, he would turn to disciple the Gentiles. (**Romans 1:16**) If Paul had a plan to evangelize the first-century world, we also need a strategic plan to evangelize our planet and its colleges.

Paul's strategy that evangelized Asia (present-day Turkey) in two years was campus ministry! (**Acts 19:8-10**) Although it is not exactly known who the "Tyrannus" of the Lecture Hall of Tyrannus was, some scholars think it was the name of a Rabbi or a man after whom the building was named. It is clear that this was a place where students learned, and it was not uncommon for teachers to rent buildings where they lectured their ideas for a set time. Interestingly, in other manuscripts, the Western text adds to verse nine, *"from the fifth hour to the tenth,"* meaning eleven o'clock in the morning until four in the afternoon.[12] Assuming "Tyrannus" owned the building, this would mean that Paul rented this building from Tyrannus during the off-peak hours of the day. Therefore, Paul believed in being a "student organization" on campus in our modern vernacular. After the higher-profile teaching was done, Paul would have just been getting done with his professional work of making tents, as Paul was not working full-time for the church at this point. The class was over now, and Paul would take advantage of this location as a place to preach the gospel.

---

12 "Tyrannus" E. Bible, Bible Gateway, accessed July 6, 2022, https://www.bible-gateway.com/resources/encyclopedia-of-the-bible/Tyrannus.

We must do as Paul did and *"make the most of every opportunity"* **(Ephesians 5:16)** on our college campuses. From this "campus ministry" at Tyrannus, disciples would evangelize all of Asia in only two years! The Book of Revelation was written to the churches of Asia, listing seven of them in chapters two and three: Ephesus (where Tyrannus was!), Smyrna, Pergamum, Thyatira, Sardis, Philadelphia, and Laodicea. There were even more than seven, as Colossae and Hierapolis were in Asia as well. **(Colossians 4:13)** This rapid expansion is the type of impact God intends to have through campus ministry. Paul did something spectacular by being consistent for two whole years in specific spiritual disciplines that this book will outline. Let us dissect this passage and unlock the keys to building a thriving army of disciples on your college campus. It first starts with you deciding to enter into campus ministry and lead!

CHAPTER 3

PAUL ENTERED—
EXEMPLARY LEADERSHIP

PAUL ENTERED—it may seem like a minor point to draw from just two words at the beginning of our Tyrannus passage, but the truth is if Paul had not gone there, nothing would have happened. Many years ago, I heard an evangelist make a straightforward yet profound point, "If you do nothing, nothing will happen." He sarcastically teased his audience about writing that down in their notes, and as funny and evident as it may sound, we may sometimes think that God will build a campus ministry on His own while we sit back and watch. It is not that God could not do that, but instead, He has chosen to limit Himself to work through the faith of men and women. We are stewards of His grace and are expected to share it with others. Jesus, Himself reveals this through the parables of the tenants and minas. In the Parable of the Ten Minas, the king goes away, giving each of his servants money with the expectation that there is a return on the capital. (**Luke 19:11-27**) The Parable of the Tenants shows the same principle, where tenants are entrusted to work in the owner's vineyard to produce the fruit of God's Kingdom. (**Matthew 21:33-43**)

Jesus has ascended to heaven and calls us to invest in other people by making disciples. God will not do it for us, but through our faith in His power and our hard work, we can yield an incredible return of souls for His glory. We are the sowers of the seed, and God will reap what we sow when He returns, but if no one sows, nothing will grow. (**Luke 19:22-23**) This is where leadership makes all the difference in building a fruitful ministry. Your campus ministry will only be as great as the quality and spirituality of its leadership. If Paul had not come to Ephesus, Asia would not have been evangelized, and the seven churches of **Revelation 2-3** indeed would not have been in existence. What type of man was Paul that made him ready to "enter" into campus ministry? Let us examine the life and character of Paul so we can imitate him and be ready to enter our respective "Halls of Tyrannus."

STRICT TRAINING

"Do you not know that in a race all the runners run, but only one gets the prize? Run in such a way as to get the prize. Everyone who competes in the games goes into strict training. They do it to get a crown that will not last, but we do it to get a crown that will last forever. Therefore I do not run like someone running aimlessly; I do not fight like a boxer beating the air. No, I strike a blow to my body and make it my slave so that after I have preached to others, I myself will not be disqualified for the prize."

-1 CORINTHIANS 9:24-27

Paul draws inspiration from the Isthmian Games that were well known in Corinth and compares the Christian life to a race. This passage has always hit home for me, having run track competitively in both high school and college, qualified and placed at a state level, and raced in the AAU Junior Olympics. Any runner understands that if you want the prize, you must go into strict training.

To win the campus ministry race, the campus leader must impose a rigorous training regimen on his personal life. The Holy Spirit says to run as if only one gets the prize. In track, only one can take first place. No athlete runs to get third or second; they train and run to get first! Unlike track, though, many people will make it to heaven, but it does not change the fact that Paul says to live this life as if only one person can make it to heaven. Paul is challenging us to tap into our competitive side to give our all in our Christianity. To build a campus ministry, you must have this runner's mindset to never give up and do your "dead-set best" at everything.

Eric Liddell was a religious Scotsman in the early 1900s who could have won the Olympics in the 100-meter dash because he had previously defeated the person who ended up winning the gold medal. The reason Liddell did not compete was that the preliminary heats for the 100-meter dash were held on Sunday. His religious conviction was that Sunday was to honor God, and therefore he pulled out. Even though the 400-meter dash was not his typical event, he chose to compete in this race, since it was held on a different day. To everyone's surprise, he won the event. Many thought he would burn out, having run the first 200-meters in a full-out sprint. Liddell was later quoted as saying, "I ran the first 200 meters as fast as I could, and with God's help, I ran the second 200 meters faster."

Often campus ministers must imitate Liddell's strategy: running the second "half" faster than the first and not giving up when tired. Campus ministry requires the same surprising amount of effort, ultimately relying on God's help to win the spiritual race.

One of the most challenging track events for me was the 400-meter dash, as I was no Eric Liddell. It is an all-out sprint, running as fast as you can for one lap around the track! Runners are familiar with hitting what is called "the wall." As you cruise around the track at full blast, the first 300 meters can seem like you are going at the speed of light; all your power, energy, stamina, and strength can then be sapped in a flash as you feel like you are hitting an invisible wall. At that point, you must dig down even deeper, start driving your arms even harder, and mentally stay determined to break through "the wall" to sprint the last hundred yards to victory.

The 4x400-meter relay was another race I ran that was the same as described above but with four others on your team. Each runner runs one lap, carrying a baton that then is handed off to the next runner. I was always the first leg or last, being one of the fastest runners. Coming around to that last 100-meters and breaking through that wall was hard. What motivated me was first the crowd and second my father being there cheering me on. I wanted to make my father proud and win one for the team. In the same way, we will blast through the campus ministry "walls" by remembering that we are surrounded by a great "crowd of witnesses" (**Hebrews 12:1-2**), our Heavenly Father is cheering us on, and we are on the greatest team—God's church!

Campus ministry has many "walls" that you will hit, but it is in those moments that you must push even harder and not quit. It is when we hit "the walls" in our ministry that our discipleship and faith are proven genuine or not. So many times, when all seems lost, and we cannot push any harder, the victory is right around the corner: *"So do not throw away your confidence; it will be richly rewarded. You need to persevere so that when you have done the will of God, you will receive what He has promised."* **(Hebrews 10:35-36)** The miracle comes right after it has been the hardest; we need to persevere, realizing we have entered strict training. A woman giving birth to a child is tempted to quit amid the labor pains! However, they persevere, and when the child is born, the miracle outweighs any pain. As the old saying goes, "No pain, no gain!"

Maybe you are reading this book because you have lost all hope, feeling you are at a standstill in your ministry. You need to persevere and drive your arms even harder in this spiritual race! Are you ready for long hours with little results? To study the Bible with hundreds of students and have many turn their back on the faith? To have baptisms and see some of them walk away from God? If so, you are ready to embark on the adventure of campus ministry! Maybe that does not sound inspiring, but I guarantee that the glory of this high-impact ministry, which God will build through you, will outweigh the hardships if you persevere.

Do not give up, my brothers and sisters! Decide today to enter the strict training of God and persevere. To not be disqualified from the prize after preaching to others, Paul beat his body and made it his slave. Remember, Paul was in Ephesus arguing persuasively for three months with seemingly few initial results except persecution before he went to Tyrannus. **(Acts 19:8-10)** His strict training mentally and physically contributed to his determined spirit to keep going. Rigorous training and self-discipline are necessary to make it to heaven and even more so to build a thriving ministry. What type of strict training does one need to impose on his life to succeed at campus ministry? The following are a few life-changing practicals to get you started.

GET RADICAL WITH GOD

Before getting into the practicals, we need to understand that anything we build will be in vain if it isn't done through God. **(Psalm 127:1)** Regardless of your role in the church, anyone venturing into building a campus ministry must have a radical relationship with God. Developing this intimacy with God requires the same determination described above but now applied to our prayer life. The Scripture says to make every effort to add to our faith. **(2 Peter 1:5-9)**

A campus intern needs to have grand, global, and earth-shaking prayers to demolish the spiritual strongholds at their colleges. As Dr. John Causey, the leader of our fast-growing sister church in Chicago, says, "You need to move God to move the ministry!" We need divine assistance. Building a ministry on our own strength will result in spiritual burnout and many who fall away from God. Scripture is clear that we plant and water, but it is God who makes the ministry grow; that we are God's co-workers. **(1 Corinthians 3:5-9)**

It is important that you find your "altar" on campus where you can retreat to pray. An "altar" was a place in the Bible where men would go to meet with God. While at Arizona State University, I found a parking garage where I would go to the top level to pray. There were never any cars parked up there, and I could overlook the campus and see the beautiful Arizona mountains. It allowed me to pour out my heart to God and implore him to work at my college. You could also pray around your campus in the morning. The point is to get radical in your relationship with God and find a place of prayer.

GET A PLANNER

The campus minister, intern, or leader who desires to advance his campus for Christ forcefully must have both the discipline and structure in their life that facilitate a strong relationship with God. Take a day at the beginning of the week on Sunday or Monday and have a discipleship time with yourself (and with your wife if you are married) to plan out the week. Ensure that, as a priority, you schedule enough time before you get to campus to have an excellent morning devotional with God. If you must work a part-time job to make ends meet, schedule enough time to have your Quiet Time before you start your shift. Then schedule your studies with non-Christians, time on campus for evangelism, church meetings, kingdom dates, academic studies, etc., with intentionality and purpose to advance God's Kingdom on your campus.

When God created mankind, two of the greatest gifts bestowed to humanity, outside of our salvation and the Holy Spirit, were free will and the ability to work. Remarkably, Adam and Eve could choose to follow God or not. His charge to them was to work the garden, but they chose to go their own way and forfeited Paradise. In the same way, God gives us the charge to make disciples of all nations. As His holy farmers, we can choose obedience and experience the blessing of God's harvest or disobedience and produce the thorns and thistles in a land in danger of being cursed. **(Genesis 3:17-19; Hebrews 6:7-8)**

Paul also spoke of himself as an *"expert builder"* when talking about his ministry. **(1 Corinthians 3:10 NIV 1984)** He consistently chose to work hard for God and boasted of sleepless nights. **(2 Corinthians 6:5 NIV 2011)** Did you know that if you decided today you wanted to pilot a plane, you could study now for the next six weeks and get your pilot's license? Six weeks from now, you could be flying a plane. It is true...but only if you schedule the time! Now this book is not about flying planes but about building campus ministries. This example shows us that where we focus our time determines the results we see in our lives and ministries.

There is an observable phenomenon in life that could be called the "law of focus." The idea is: What we focus on expands. For example, if you drove around and I told you to focus on all the red cars, all of a sudden you would notice more red cars than you ever did before. The red vehicles would expand in your vision. We often think there is no one "open to the gospel" because we focus on the negative rather than setting our minds to focus on open people. When you have a focus, it expands your perspective. My point is if you focus on being a dedicated campus worker, your campus work will grow. Do not underestimate the power of setting your mind on the work God has given you to do.

One of the biggest challenges we have is consistency. A pilot's license, a school degree, or a building project are each completed with strict training, diligence, focus, and ultimately—consistency. Someone once said, "The most radical thing you can do is be consistent."

Your schedule is where consistency is implemented and where one becomes the architect of life and ministry. You have the freedom to build a schedule that can, in turn, create a thriving campus ministry. Whatever you schedule consistently is going to determine and impact the results in your ministry.

"Family time" is a planned time to build closeness and connection in your campus ministry. If I plan family time with the disciples every week, the result will be a close-knit fellowship in my ministry. Sharing time is where the campus ministry goes out and evangelizes the lost. If I schedule time to reach out to non-Christians every week in my ministry, the result will be tons of new Bible studies consistently in my ministry. Again, if you do nothing, nothing will happen, but you will see results if you build a schedule for success.

To grow the ministry numerically, it is essential to schedule most of your available time with non-Christians. Jesus was known as someone who spent time with tax collectors and sinners. **(Mark 2:13-17)** If we are to be like Jesus, we must schedule our time with the lost. This could look like Bible studies, life talks, shooting pool, or playing sports on campus. Just remember: More time with non-Christians equals more baptisms! Time is your most precious commodity as a disciple and the reason why you need an effective planning system. Another ministry admonition from Dr. John Causey is, "Move the ministry week to week so God can grow it month to month."

Maybe the disciples in your ministry continuously want to hang out exclusively with each other. This happens as good-hearted Christians enjoy the fellowship of the kingdom so much. As the campus worker, you must create a culture that pulls non-Christians into these hang-out times. Often, we think of sharing our faith as only going out canvassing on campus. Do not forget the opportunities we have to share our faith by inviting non-Christians to fellowship times. We often forget that sharing our faith should be fun—more on this later!

All your Bible studies should be set up at the beginning of the week, with enough time left to schedule the next studies. The focus needs to be on the "hot studies." A hot study is a study with an open-hearted individual willing to move forward in the Bible studies and embrace the challenges given him from God's Word. Alternatively, it is a study with a potential leader (opinion leader) who needs the special attention of the campus minister and generally takes more time to make Jesus Lord. In your planning time, you want to look through all your Bible studies and determine which ones are either the most open or the most influential. The campus minister or intern wants to put themselves in the most open-hearted studies to generate more baptisms. It is also crucial to "jump in" the studies with opinion leaders to convert more leaders.

In my planning time, I try to schedule all my "hot studies" on Monday or Tuesday, leaving free time to set up the following studies with those people Wednesday or Thursday. Disciples need to be trained to bring people who are studying to church and immediately after service, set them up to study the Bible early in the week, striking while the iron is hot. The iron is hot because after hearing a riveting sermon, experiencing sincere worship, and feeling the love of the fellowship, they are thinking spiritually about their lives. It is the perfect time to ask them what they thought about the sermon and set up a Bible study. The Apostle John recalled a lesson Jesus taught on evangelism where He told His disciples to open their eyes to all the ripened fruit around them; he was urgently showing them they must reap while the fruit was ripe. **(John 4:34-35)** If a farmer took too long to reap, the fruit could quickly become rotten because he missed the opportunity. Paul never missed an opportunity to pick the ripe fruit; he was alert, calculated, and precise! As he reminded the Corinthians about the importance of strict training, he reminded them that he did not run aimlessly or *"fight like a boxer beating the air."* **(1 Corinthians 9:26)** Your schedule must be focused and made to produce results.

No matter how great the schedule or how filled up the planner is, it will mean nothing if the schedule is not obeyed. Again, if you do nothing, nothing happens! Once your schedule is made, you must be obedient to your schedule. For the plan to work, you must work the plan. Sometimes it is hardest for us to obey ourselves, so Paul said he made his body his slave. Of course, life throws curve balls at us; people cancel and reschedule meetings, our church staff may need us for a task, etc. Jesus always had people interjecting themselves into His life (lepers, the bleeding woman, etc.). Yet, He did not allow it to pull Him away from His mission. He saw these events as great opportunities to advance His mission and bring glory to God. Determine to become a master of your schedule while being able to surrender to God's sovereignty in that which you cannot control.

It is essential to consider what needs to be removed from your schedule. If you want to build a growing campus ministry, everything in your schedule must contribute to that cause. Everything you do should directly or indirectly contribute to the growth of your campus ministry. For example, although it may be fun to go to the new Chemical Recovery ministry your church started, that is precious time away from your call to work your campus, unless you do need recovery yourself. That is just one distracting example of many. Maybe you want to do a financial workshop to help everyone in your ministry. That is noble, but if you are the campus minister, let someone else do it. You must have 100% of your heart focused on the growth of your campus. Activity often replaces productivity when we schedule good and even spiritual things that do not directly contribute to our campus ministry's growth.

God has called you to build the campus ministry, not other ministries. Of course, you must schedule a time to replenish, have fun, and go on dates; however, they should not dominate your schedule. Perhaps you spend too much time playing video games, going on social media, or watching movies. What are areas of your schedule not helping you build your campus ministry that need to be removed? Take some time to consider this question and ask the Holy Spirit to clarify whether the ministries you are participating in are distractions to building up your campus. I would encourage church leaders not to have their campus workers doing teen ministry, children's ministry, or any other specialized ministry. The work of campus ministry requires the total devotion of the campus worker. It also requires spiritual focus and an undivided heart. Later in this book, we will expound on the concepts briefly mentioned in this section. Another crucial area of strict training necessary to prepare ourselves to enter the campus ministry is our purity.

GET PURITY

Paul says, *"... [he] beat his body and made it his slave so that after he preached to others he would not be disqualified from the prize."* (**1 Corinthians 9:27**) The campus worker must have a strong walk with God and personal integrity to prevent him from Satan's schemes. He or she must have firm personal boundaries regarding their purity and work with the opposite sex. A whole book could be written on the importance of this topic—even more so on campus, where sexual impurity is lurking at every turn. I would personally encourage every male campus worker to read Dr. Raul Moreno's book, *A Battle That Even King's Lost,* on overcoming sexual impurity. Being in campus ministry in different capacities for many years of my life, I can attest to the growing impurity on campus through social media, pornography, the "Selfie Generation," and the progressive immodesty of dress. Campus leaders are always surrounded by temptations that demand extra measures to protect their walk with God in this area since they are on campus almost all day.

I made many mistakes as a single campus minister that brought about God's loving discipline during my life in my early years in campus ministry. There was even a time when my impurity threatened my calling as a minister. It is only by His grace that God granted me repentance and that I sit here happily married, leading in God's Kingdom and writing this book. The keys I am going to share with you are guidelines I wish I had as deep convictions in my early campus ministry days. Thank God for the discipling I received and the experiences I had that instilled the convictions that now protect me from crossing inappropriate lines.

"Likewise, teach the older women to be reverent in the way they live, not to be slanderers or addicted to much wine, but to teach what is good. Then they can urge the younger women to love their husbands and children, to be self-controlled and pure, to be busy at home, to be kind, and to be subject to their husbands, so that no one will malign the word of God. Similarly, encourage the young men to be self-controlled. In everything set them an example by doing what is good. In your teaching show integrity, seriousness and soundness of speech that cannot be condemned, so that those who oppose you may be ashamed because they have nothing bad to say about us."

-TITUS 2:3-8

"Do not rebuke an older man harshly, but exhort him as if he were your father. Treat younger men as brothers, older women as mothers, and younger women as sisters, with absolute purity."

-1 TIMOTHY 5:1-2

It is clear from the Scriptures above that the women are to be discipled, counseled, and taught by the older women and the men discipled and taught by the men. The brothers must entrust the women's ministry to the women, especially when it comes to the younger women involved in your campus ministry. Interactions with the opposite sex must be above reproach. The best practices for building a culture of purity in campus ministry must start with hardline convictions. The campus worker must never be alone with the opposite sex in any circumstance. Even now, as a married man, if I must give a woman a ride home after a church event, I have her sit in the back of my car while I am driving. The men should study the Bible with men, and women should study the Bible with women. The only situation in which a brother leader may get involved in a women's Bible study or counseling situation is when the woman is having challenges with doctrine that do not include emotional issues. Still, even then, another Christian woman should be present in the study with them.

The International Christian Churches have a fantastic custom that has helped honor God in our college ministries' standard of purity. We encourage the church members to go on "friendship dates" or "encouragement times" with other Christians on the weekends. These are dates Christians can ask each other on, then plan a fun activity, and double date with another couple. It does not mean there is a romantic interest but is merely fulfilling the Scripture in **Hebrews 3:12-14** that says we should encourage one another to guard our hearts against the deceptiveness of sin. The truth is that Christian men are tempted continuously by the rampant immodesty on campus, and Christian women are regularly hit on by men in the world. By creating an atmosphere where Christians are encouraged to go on fun double dates with each other on the weekends, the hearts of the disciples are protected from temptation. The students are taught to build godly, healthy relationships with the opposite sex.

Single campus leaders need to be going on Christian encouragement dates every weekend to encourage those in the campus ministry. This is the only time the campus leader should be building friendships with the opposite sex in a focused manner. All other time should be devoted to being laser-focused on advancing the ministry. Jesus said, *"But seek first His Kingdom and His righteousness and all these things will be given to you as well."* (**Matthew 6:33**) This single-minded focus of time may seem extreme for some, but the Bible is clear we should treat the opposite sex as if they were our physical siblings. (**1 Timothy 5:2**) The campus workers must go above and beyond to guard their hearts in these matters. (**Proverbs 4:23**) Besides, when they are focused on God and building the ministry, they do not have time to sin or get distracted by the opposite sex. They trust God has a plan for them and will provide in His timing. Creating a culture in your campus ministry in which the disciples look forward to pure dating on Saturday nights will help them stay focused on advancing God's work during the week.

GET (LOTS OF) TIME ON CAMPUS

We saw earlier that even though Paul worked a secular job, he was finished by eleven in the morning to go to the Lecture Hall of Tyrannus and have daily discussions (what we would call Bible Talks). A Bible Talk is a small group Bible discussion focused on evangelizing students on campus. They can take place in the cafeteria, outside, or in the dormitories. The Bible Talk leader comes up with a spiritual discussion based on a passage of Scripture. Most of the campus worker's time should be focused on inviting students to such discussions. The college campus must become your office. The key for the leader is to spend as much time on campus as possible. From my experience, there is nothing that produces more results than the time you spend on campus.

Traveling to Phoenix, Arizona, fresh out of college to lead my first campus ministry at the nation's largest university at the time (Arizona

State University), I was filled with excitement and vision. My mind-set was if ASU was the largest college population in the nation (at the time competing with Ohio State University), we should have one of the nation's largest campus ministries. I made a quick stop in Los Angeles and had the privilege to speak to a hero in the faith, Dr. Kip McKean, getting his advice on how to go about building the campus ministry in Phoenix.

Kip is known for building discipling ministries that spread expo-nentially around the world. A large part of his God-given success came from the lessons he learned as a campus minister in his early days. In the small town of Charleston, Illinois, he took a group of seven students and saw some 300 students baptized in three years! The advice he gave me has stayed with me to this day.

Kip's advice was simple but challenging, and the fruit that would come in our future ministries validated his wisdom. He shared he would enjoy his mornings having a powerful Quiet Time, and sleep in if he needed to (which surprised me at the time) but made sure he would be on campus by eleven in the morning every day. He would then spend all day on campus and not come home until eleven at night. Eleven to eleven was his method! His goal was to become known as the campus minister at whatever college or university he was at. Kip advised me to have all my appointments on campus, take my meals on campus, write my sermons on campus, and if possible, live right by campus. Kip's overall conviction was crystal clear; there is no shortcut to the principle of maximizing time on campus.

Over the years I have also learned that campus workers may need to work an early morning job from 4:00 AM until noon or a night-shift job to pay the bills and get more time on campus if they do not yet work for the church. One of the most effective campus ministers I knew worked at Starbucks early in the morning and would get off work around noon to be on campus by early afternoon. The principle was clear for me, eleven to eleven or noon to midnight is what it takes to build a thriving college ministry! The old saying goes, "Time is money," but in campus ministry, "Time is baptisms!"

The author will never forget Kip McKean's crucial advice to stay on campus all day to move the ministry forward.

GET STUDENTS TO LEAD

Now that we have established the spiritual mindset about individual boundaries and time commitments that the campus leader must embrace, it is time to share the final principle of this chapter:

Student leadership. It should go without saying that students are the key to reaching other students. Many campus ministries that are brand new are started by a single or a young married couple or maybe even a student who does not go to that college. If you are beginning a brand-new campus ministry and have no enrolled students, you and those you are bringing on campus must become part of the school's fabric. Blending in and knowing the campus well is essential, especially if you are starting a campus ministry from scratch—more on that later. For now, if you do have enrolled students, you must focus on developing them into leaders.

To help your college students to grow as leaders, you want them to lead Bible Talks, preach at devotionals, disciple new Christians, and be actively involved in the local church congregation. Although evangelistic campaigns and cold-contact evangelism have varying degrees of effectiveness, your most powerful evangelism tool for reaching more for Christ is the enrolled student disciple. They are frequently in classes, clubs, and sports; usually living in or near the college; and already have a circle of friends they can bring into the kingdom.

Enrolled campus disciples are also your key to becoming a student organization at the university. You must emphasize in your preaching and teaching the call to reach out to their classmates, peers, professors, and friends. At Boston University, one of the sisters who was a student reached out to her African Studies professor. She came around the church for almost a year, studied the Bible, and was victoriously baptized into Christ! Another brother who served as a house church leader taught as a professor at Berklee College of Music in Boston. Not surprisingly, he had been very fruitful in converting college students to Christ because of his college position.

Early on leading his first campus ministry at Arizona State University,
the author always answered an inquisitive young Christian, Elizabeth
McDonnell's Bible questions. She would marry a fiery young
disciple from the same campus ministry, Richie McDonnell,
and lead churches in Washington, DC; Manila,
Philippines; and Minneapolis, MN.

GET STARTED FROM SCRATCH

If you are in a situation where you do not have any students on
campus, you are in the same situation Paul usually was in! Most likely,
Paul met his twelve guys in Ephesus. (**Acts 19:1-5**) It is believed that

these same twelve who were "rebaptized" in this passage are the disciples he later took to the campus to start that ministry that evangelized Asia.

You will need to spend most of your time doing cold-contact evangelism. There is no shortcut or secret to creating a ministry from scratch other than a total commitment to cold-contact evangelism. Minimally, you will need to share your faith with 50 to 100 people a day. One out of ten people invited to Bible Talk or church service will be open to coming. That one may be open to studying the Bible. Then, depending on their heart, they possibly might get baptized. Therefore, you must share your faith with hundreds of people every week if you hope to make an impact. Raul Moreno, who built a premier campus ministry in Sao Paolo, says it takes ten Bible studies for one student to get baptized. After you convert your first couple of students, you can begin to put them to work. You must have the conviction that you need to talk with "tons" of new people every day. There are no shortcuts to this. The more people with whom you share your faith, the more who will potentially get baptized.

I want to emphasize the word "potentially" because God ultimately determines the results. **(1 Corinthians 3:6-7)** After taking a semester break from my college studies to work a secular job, I had the opportunity to work in sales telemarketing for a phone company. It was an incredible job with a base salary and commission on the sales that were made. On top of that, there was a very competitive, yet fun corporate culture that was enhanced by all the awards that could be added to your commissions. The strategy was simple: Make as many cold calls as possible to businesses attempting to sell our product to them. To my shock, the phone company had a surprising turnover of employees. There were constantly new employees coming in to work in our cubicle. Why would people quit such a fantastic job? I could not understand.

Simply put, they could not handle the constant rejection—being told no, hang-ups, being cursed out, etc. Only those who understood it was simply getting through large numbers of potential customers to find those receptive to the product were the ones who succeeded majorly in the company and lasted for the long haul. The only way to fail at this job was to make too few calls or quit altogether from discouragement. God used this job to teach me a lot about people, deal with large amounts of rejection, and forcefully advance the ministry through perseverance.

As disciples, we experience a similar rejection when someone is not open to our message. Unlike sales, the rejection is more painful because we offer them eternal life and not just a phone plan! Remember what Jesus taught in these moments: They reject Jesus and not you. (**John 15:20**) Not taking rejection personally but surrendering it to Jesus is crucial to starting a campus ministry from scratch. The danger is in getting discouraged. Discouragement can result in pulling back your heart and limiting the number of people with whom you share your faith. Satan starts to deceive us into thinking that no one is open, a direct contradiction to the Scriptures that teach the harvest is plentiful. (**Matthew 9:35-38**) There are multitudes of open people, but only a few workers; basic statistics tell us that those few workers will have to share with a lot of people to find all the open ones. Surprisingly few men and women are willing to put in the hard work to grow their ministry. How hard will you work for the Lord?

Campus ministry is all about doing something! In physics, inertia is defined as "the resistance of any physical object to any change in its state of motion (this includes changes to its speed, direction, or state of rest)." Objects tend to keep moving in a straight line at a constant velocity. When launching a rocket, it takes more fuel (up to 30%) to move the rocket the first twelve inches than any other time in the flight! In the same way, if you want your campus ministry to take off, the leader must put enough force to overcome inertia and create momentum in the ministry. *Paul entered,* momentum was generated, and a Jesus Movement began in Asia! Paul believed his presence made a difference. At one point, he said he would rather go to heaven, but it would be better for the Philippian church for him to stay on earth, which would mean fruitful labor for him and consequently for the whole church! Paul believed his effort mattered—that he was an X factor in forceful advancement! **(Philippians 1:22-26)**

It is time for you to enter your campus and have the same kind of impact! This is done by building personal integrity into your schedule, maintaining excellent purity, and committing to massive amounts of time on campus while focusing on finding and raising up student leadership. Take time to reflect on the principles in this chapter. Are you prepared in these areas? If so, it is time to get ready to speak boldly!

CHAPTER 4

SPOKE BOLDLY—
CAMPUS PRESENCE

Speaking at the SAGES (South Asia Gulf and the Eastern States)
Campus Conference at Florida International University.

PAUL SPOKE BOLDLY AND PERSUASIVELY. Today, there is so much false doctrine and secular humanism stemming from intellectual pride on our college campuses. Paul combatted similar problems with his strong preaching, which established the presence of the kingdom of God on the "campus" of his day. Disciples in our campus ministries must have leaders like Paul, who not only know how to preach boldly but who can also train others to do the same and therefore establish God's church wherever they go. Creating a powerful campus presence takes the following: Establishing your group as an official student organization, holding dynamic devotionals that provide opportunities for you and your students to preach and have fun, and training your student leaders through powerful campus leadership meetings.

BECOMING A STUDENT ORGANIZATION

Devotionals should be done on the college campus. Most public universities offer the opportunity for students to become a club or student organization on campus. One of the advantages of being a student organization is that you can rent rooms on campus for devotionals. Student organizations are allowed to have marketing or "tabling events" set up in high-traffic areas on campus, hand out invites for events, and even receive money for ministry events from the student government. Finally, being a student organization brings legitimacy to your ministry in the eyes of those whom you are trying to persuade.

There are only a few hurdles to overcome in becoming a club, and they can differ from university to university, country to country. First, you must put together a constitution. The college will usually have a sample constitution and specific guidelines depending on the campus at which you are located. This handbook will provide a sample constitution you can use in the appendix. Next, you need a president, vice president, treasurer, and secretary. The college sometimes requires ten or so signatures of students who are "members" of the club. In God's church, these roles mean nothing as they are not biblical or church-recognized offices. Whoever fills these roles does not matter, except that the president should be a disciple or close friend since they will be the one who makes your room reservations. If the number of disciples is too small, you can enlist students friendly towards the church or who have studied the Bible in the past to fill these roles. Depending on the college, they may have more specific requirements.

Perhaps the most challenging obstacle is finding an advisor for your club. An advisor is usually a professor at a college or university. Use students in your campus ministry or students you know to talk to professors they are close to about becoming the club advisor. They usually do not have to do anything except sign a piece of paper. In most cases, you do not want them to be overly involved or to take an active leadership role since most likely they are not a disciple of Jesus and will have conflicting views and ideas. Ideally, you want full leadership authority of the group. An advisor could also be sought through cold contact. Look for a professor who is friendly towards "Christianity." It is essential to remind the student or students who reserve rooms for you on campus to remember important student organization meetings they must attend as club officers and keep the club up to date with paperwork and requirements. I have seen situations in which a simple appointment was missed, online paperwork was not submitted on time, and the group ceased to be a recognized student organization.

It cannot be emphasized how important it is to become a campus club, if possible. It puts your ministry on the map as a force right in the heart of the college. If you cannot become a club on campus for some reason, you should still have campus devotional as close as possible. Look into how much it costs non-clubs to rent rooms on campus and talk to your evangelist or church leader.

Another option to research is becoming a "Religious Life Advisor" at your college. Luke Speckman, who formally led the New York International Christian Church, investigated this and was able to become a Religious Life Advisor at the prestigious Columbia University. Even though we were already a student organization there, it created even more legitimacy and opportunity. For example, they let our entire church (students and non-students) meet on campus for Wednesday Midweeks in the St. Paul's Chapel. Luke is required to be on campus for a few hours a week, and he can study the Bible with students in his own office, or students can come to him for spiritual advice. Rafael Jerez, who used to lead the Syracuse church, could not initially help his campus group become a student organization at Syracuse University. However, imitating Luke's example, he became a Religious Life Advisor. Becoming an advisor helped legitimize this traditionally persecuted campus ministry while also giving them access to meeting spaces.

One of the reasons you may find it hard to become a Christian club on campus is that most colleges already have tons of "Christian" clubs. When I was the campus minister at the University of Central Florida, there were over 50 "Christian" student organizations already established on campus! It was hard to become a club for years on this campus because they wanted to know what made this group different from the other groups. Rest assured, the college was not concerned with doctrine. Despite having radically different doctrinal views when you hold to the Bible, the college wants to know what makes the group's activities and purposes different from the other "Christian" organizations. I will forever be grateful to Anthony Eckels, who came up with the idea of becoming an art club on campus that emphasizes faith. Becoming an art club is a route you can take if they do not allow you to become a "Christian club." You can also become an AMS (Arts, Media, and Sports) club. *Merriam-Webster* defines "art" as a *skill acquired by experience, study, or observation.* Of course, we study the Bible and sing songs that fall under this definition and others! The point is, do not give up because one door closes. I cannot overemphasize how important it is that you become a recognized student organization on campus.

One of our campus ministry names and logos started at the
University of Central Florida, based on Colossians 2:17,
which teaches that "reality is found in Christ."

FRIDAY NIGHTS

Campus Devotional is a time for the college ministry to come together as a family. The timing of Campus Devotional is intentionally chosen to protect the students from the temptations present on Friday nights. Most college students are partying, drinking, and destroying their lives on Friday nights. It is therefore important that devotionals are lively and fun to compete with the worldly parties going on. The devotional is not predominantly a time to preach to visitors or non-Christians. This is the purpose of Bible Talk and Sunday church services. That is not to say you cannot bring visitors to devotionals, but you are focusing on equipping the disciples during this time. It is the one shot you can get as a campus leader to address your campus ministry's issues and needs directly. What the "huddle" is to a sports team, so is the devotional to your campus "team:" a time to prepare your team for the next play and to coach them on what they could improve from the week before. Devotionals should be guided and focused to bring the ministry closer to God and accomplish the goals of the ministry.

PREACHING

Now that you are a legitimate group on campus or can meet right by the college for your devotional, what should you preach? Campus devotional is the perfect opportunity to preach lessons on relevant topics that disciples in college face. These sermons should focus on practical application. This time is also an excellent opportunity to train the student leaders you are raising up to preach. The appendix has devotional sermon outlines you can use to make into your own and preach. Topics of importance for campus ministry are not limited to, but include: Evangelism, purity, dating, persecution, purity, persecution, oh, and did I mention purity and persecution? In all seriousness, one of the topics I consistently call my campus leaders to preach about is persecution. There is no other ministry that gets as much persecution from family and friends as the campus ministry. **2 Timothy 3:12** promises persecution to those who live a godly life. Your preaching will equip the students with the right attitude and the proper perspective to view persecution. Your teaching can also help students manage their reputation on campus by being wise and discreet and avoiding unwarranted persecution. Purity is another topic you will have to preach about repeatedly, including the purpose of double-dating and the standards disciples of Jesus are to hold in this area. (**Ephesians 5:3-7**)

Zeal accomplishes a great deal when it comes to campus ministry. (**Isaiah 9:7**) The Campus Minister or campus leader needs to be an example of zeal. You also want to preach and carry yourself in a way that can be followed and imitated by your student leaders. (**1 Corinthians 11:1**) The Bible commands us to never be lacking in zeal. (**Romans 12:11**) To be lacking in zeal is to sin against God. The professors and students at your university are passionate about changing the world in their way. Passion is contagious and can change the whole atmosphere of a room. Your walk with God needs to be emotional, deep, and radical as this is the source of your passion. Does your presence change the atmosphere at a devotional?

A typical devotional can be structured with powerful singing, a welcome, good news sharing or prayer requests, announcements, more singing, a sermon, and open response. These sections of the devotional provide opportunities for more students to participate. To learn more about putting together a devotional sermon, you could listen to my lesson, "How To Put Together A Sermon."[13] The key is to preach passionately and with deep conviction.

It is imperative to have not only preaching devotionals but also family-building events and worship devotionals. Worship devotionals

---

13 Mike Patterson. "How to Put a Sermon Together." Mike Patterson, 2013. YouTube Video, 1:7:27. https://youtu.be/SkhkEuRMVSw.

are a time when the disciples sing and pray for the whole duration of the meeting. Berklee College of Music, one of the top colleges for music and singing, gave the Boston Church a grant to meet on campus once a month to hold worship devotionals. Not only is this very relatable to the more religious campus students, but it also helps the disciples grow in their spirituality. Encouragingly, the college even gave funds to provide food at the worship devotional. During the time of King Jehoshaphat, the Israelites used the praise of God as their only weapon to defeat their enemies. **(2 Chronicles 20:22)** In the same way, the early Christians knew this same power of worship, as God granted them victory and added to their number even while they were praising him. **(Acts 2:47)**

Early on in my ministry career, I learned a difficult lesson: Too many members fell away because I loved preaching but did not value playing games, sports, or having fun events during devotionals. I was always focusing on the business of forcefully advancing the kingdom, which is needed. At the time, I failed to realize that having fun is part of advancing the ministry. In my mind, I just thought the emphasis on having fun was less spiritual. To me, the work of the ministry was fun! I have since learned that not everyone is like me!

Fun, food, and games are what build a family. **Acts 2:42-47** shows the early church was a family that enjoyed being with each other. Not only is the church the army of God, but also the family of God. Events must facilitate getting to know one another in the ministry. Part of why I focused every devotional on preaching and teaching early on was because I loved preaching so much. The result was many disciples felt as though "fun" had no place in the church and began to turn to the world to find "fun." If people do not have fun in the ministry, they will seek it in the world. The kingdom of God is different from the world, and we must avoid the extreme of becoming another "youth group" or "Christian club" on campus whose whole ministry is centered on "fun events" and "worship" (singing songs). Yet, at the same time, we cannot neglect fun and games. For these same reasons, people go to these other "Christian" groups on campus. Some are fun and have food and astonishing singing though they neglect the preaching of God's Word. There must be a balance between these types of family-building events and the hardline preaching of God's Word. Never forget: It is the Word of God that changes people and has a lasting impact!

Other types of devotionals I like to do center around apologetics or deeper theological topics. Students love these theological devotionals because they build confidence in the Word of God and equip them with weapons to defend against the inundation of evolutionary, philosophical, and theoretical teachings from their professors. Assembling PowerPoint presentations on what different denominations teach, creating a "Prepared to Answer" series to combat false teaching, or possibly putting together a "Proof of God" apologetics presentation goes a long way in equipping the saints to be deeply rooted in their faith. As Solomon famously wrote, *"There is a time for everything and a season for every activity under the heavens."* **(Ecclesiastes 3:1)** I believe most devotionals should involve preaching that is practical and geared toward the students and the specific needs of each campus ministry. What about the fun-night devotionals? What should one do for them?

FUN

Of course, you can never go wrong with bowling, pizza, a movie, or celebrating a member's birthday by having some food and sharing words of encouragement. These times of sharing are crucial to creating intimacy and family in the ministry. I remember one woman being so impacted by a sharing event we had for one of the disciples being sent off to another church that she studied and became a disciple! She saw the deep family in the sharing for the young man being sent off. What are some other devotional ideas that will enliven your campus ministry with fun?

One creative devotional we do here in Boston is to have a night of role-playing. I go to the front and act like a non-Christian or a weak disciple. I then invite the campus disciples to come up and help me, using the Bible. I would call on the different disciples and throw situations at them in which they had to use the Bible to help me become a Christian, help me grow spiritually, or refute my false doctrine. I might say, "I do not see in the Bible why we have to go to Midweek Service or Friday Devotional." The student would then have to use the Bible on the spot to disciple me. This role-playing helps those watching who are in the weak situations being acted out to be convicted by the Bible and learn the biblical convictions behind why we do what we do as a congregation. Bible jeopardy is always fun and, at times, can become very competitive and team-building. Putting together skits on how to share your faith in cold contact situations with people on your campus equips the students and can be very humorous.

Any effective ministry must be devoted to prayer. Notice that Luke records that prayer comes first before ministry in the Book of Acts.

(**Acts 6:4**) All-night prayer nights are powerful times to energize the disciples spiritually. These can be done before the start of a new semester. You can also have a prayer devotional to teach the disciples how to pray more powerfully and reverently; reviewing the ACTS prayer acronym is one of my favorites—Adoration, Confession, Thanksgiving, and Supplication. The campus leader teaches for a minute on "adoration," then you sing a song of adoration to God and have different people pray prayers of only praise to God. Next, the leader shares on "confession," and then you have your campus pair up with someone of the same sex and go and pray prayers of confession for an allotted time. The process continues through the acronym.

Fun events are crucial to building a campus ministry that keeps the saved, saved. The author in his campus ministry days in his gorilla costume is enjoying himself at a ministry party.

Finally, I have found that students love to dance. One event the students have come to enjoy in our fellowship is the "PURE Dance." Here, the disciples can party without the world's impurity. The DJ must play clean music, and those who express weak consciences coming from a conservative background are excused not to participate. (**Romans 14**) These devotionals keep things lively and still equip the students in their walk with God.

CAMPUS LEADERS MEETING

To run an effective campus ministry, you must run it as if it is a church. In every church, you have the church leader (usually the Lead Evangelist), a group of leaders (the men and women with whom the Evangelist and Women's Ministry Leader are in a discipling relationship), and a staff meeting (the training ground for that small discipleship group). For a very fruitful ministry, a separate campus leaders meeting is essential; it parallels the church staff meeting, allowing the campus leaders to train and raise up their key leaders.

One-man leadership is found throughout the entire Bible. Anytime God's people prospered, they had one central leader: Moses, Joshua, David, Jesus, Peter, etc. Even in the basic family unit, the husband is the leader. The same is needed in the campus ministry of every church. Sometimes I will hear of a church leader having two or three campus leaders and dividing the ministry into three groups even at the same college. Having multiple leaders on the same campus usually sets the young leaders up to feel a sense of competition towards one another and causes all kinds of dysfunction, especially if the church leader is leading the ministry from a distance. I suggest the church leader select one couple to lead the campus ministry, allowing the church leader couple to focus strictly on discipling the campus lead couple. This campus leader then needs to have his small group of campus Bible Talk leaders whom he is discipling. In a smaller church, I suggest the church leader couple also be the campus leader couple until someone can raise up into this role. This setup would mean the church leader couple would disciple the campus Bible Talk leaders or opinion leaders and delegate the singles and marrieds to a qualified couple with whom they would meet once a week to shepherd those ministries.

Now that you have your campus leadership group, this is where the campus version of "staff meeting" comes in. When I was in college, our campus minister started a Sunday night leader's meeting for the leaders he discipled within the group. He called it the "Cave of Adullam" based on the formation of David's mighty men! I felt so honored to be chosen to be a part of this special group, like one of David's mighty men! The Bible Talk I was leading at my college at the time was also held late at night on Sunday, around 8:00 PM, after a long day of church, Bible Talk Leader's Meeting, studies, and discipleship times. I later realized the late-night timing, specifically after a long day, served to train people to continue giving of themselves all day long. This type of spiritual stamina is necessary to build a growing college ministry; we need to be prepared to be tired all the time and learn how to get spiritually refreshed quickly and constantly. After a long day of giving, the disciples seemed to be more open, vulnerable, and willing to let their guards down for some excellent discipling to occur.

Most of your college ministry leaders go to the "Bible Talk Leader's Meeting" that occurs Sunday afternoon. This meeting is also essential, as it is how the Lead Evangelist of the church directly teaches and influences the Bible Talk Leaders. Yet, it is still not enough time in most cases to give specific direction and training for the campus ministry. The truth is campus Bible Talks function quite differently in many cases than those in the singles or married ministries. The reality is the campus ministry moves (or should be moving) at a much more rapid pace than any other ministry in the church. There needs to be a time the campus leader can talk confidentially to his trainees about issues in the ministry and focus on moving all the studies forward. This extra meeting in the evening allows the leader to set up the week for the campus ministry to be truly effective.

During this weekly Sunday night meeting, you should talk through the studies with non-Christians and develop a plan to lovingly "gang tackle" the person studying to bring them to a decision for Christ in the waters of baptism. During this meeting, quizzes should be given over past sermons, good news in the kingdom, general Bible knowledge, etc. This time is also useful to sharpen up your leaders' ability to teach the First Principles studies, a study series the International Christian Churches use to bring someone into a relationship with Jesus. At one point, after experiencing a period of successful numerical growth in the University of Florida Campus Ministry, I remember grabbing my campus leaders and teaching them a more intensive and quick-paced First Principles course. We met a few nights a week at my place at 10:00 PM. Having campus leaders who are trained and confident in presenting the gospel is essential in sustaining the growth of the ministry, especially after adding so many new Christians in a short time.

When I served the Lord at the University of Central Florida (UCF) in Orlando, we playfully called this Campus Leaders Meeting

"Ringleaders" based on **Acts 24:5**, which says, *"We have found this man to be a troublemaker, stirring up riots among the Jews all over the world. He is a ringleader of the Nazarene sect."* This group was invite-only, and it created a sensation in the ministry that people wanted to be a "Ringleader." Jesus, of course, did this when he called twelve men together and formed the small leadership group of the *Apostles* (literally the *Messengers).* Through these men, He would build His church, and it is through this group you will build your campus ministry. As we have studied, Paul also spoke boldly and argued persuasively in Ephesus to build his leadership base! These Campus Devotionals and Sunday Night Campus Leaders Meetings provide the opportunity to preach boldly and equip the saints for service.

After being persecuted by the Jews and not seeing many results preaching in the synagogues, Paul swiftly changed his strategy and moved his ministry to the Lecture Hall of Tyrannus. Meetings are essential if they serve a purpose, but it is now time to move to the Lecture Hall of Tyrannus with Paul's same faithful conviction and action! Have you moved to your campus in the same way Paul moved to the Lecture Hall? This must happen first and foremost on a heart level, but you also need to become a student group on campus. Do you believe college ministry is the heartbeat of the church? Have you done everything you can to become a student organization?

Living on the campus in the dorms or close by is another way to gain a presence on the campus, maximizing your impact. Would you be willing to move your housing to live closer to the college or university you are serving or to call your students to live in the dorms? Often, disciples want the comfort of living in a nicer apartment instead of student housing, and yet it is the campus leader's responsibility to help them put the mission of Christ above their own comforts.

Leading my first campus ministry at Arizona State University, I had no idea what I was doing. I just knew I had to be on campus most of the day. Following the advice of my spiritual mentors, I moved right across the street from campus, literally a three-minute walk. The accessibility made it easier to meet students and have a strong presence in the college. The temptation to go, "I don't feel like driving all the way over there," or maybe the headache of finding a parking spot is eliminated when you live near or on the campus. In addition, it allows the campus leader to serve the students by having them over for a home-cooked meal, providing the love and fellowship most college students crave when away from home for the first time. For both the campus minister and the student disciples, living on or near campus drastically increases their opportunities to preach the Word to the student population they desire to reach.

Ezekiel 37:1-10 recounts the dry bones that come to life at the preaching of Ezekiel the prophet. God shows us that preaching can bring life to any situation. In the Bible, Ezekiel's preaching brought the bones together to form a skeleton or structure for the flesh and breath. In the same way, becoming a club, having a powerful devotional, and holding a Sunday Night Campus Leaders Meeting are the bones that form the skeleton of your campus ministry, which can then be brought to life through the strong preaching of your young leaders.

It is essential to have a weekly structure that propels your ministry. Once you have that, it is time to preach what you need into existence.

Just as God spoke the world into existence, you must boldly speak your campus ministry into existence. Do you need your campus workers to move closer to the college? Preach on it! Do you need your workers not to work as much at their secular job and spend more time on campus? Preach on it! Do you need students to raise up? Preach on it!

God asked Ezekiel, "Can these bones live?" God wanted the prophet to preach believing! To preach with faith! It is interesting to me to look at different campus ministries. I have seen this skeleton of structure and activity implemented in specific campus ministries but only yield meager results. How is it possible that some have tons of fruit by applying these things and others do not? I believe the X factor is faith. You cannot replace the zeal or passion of true faith. It is the gas that gets the car moving. If you are working hard but lacking results, it is only the preaching of God's Word that can fill the disciples with the fuel of faith.

Even though Paul had his system down (first to the Jews, then to the Gentiles), he faced obstinate people, and his ministry was stuck for three months. Maybe you have the meetings and devotionals down, the skeleton is there, and you are preaching with faith but are still stuck. What do you do then?

CHAPTER 5

FOR THREE MONTHS—TURNING AROUND A DEAD CAMPUS MINISTRY

The author's first campus ministry he led at Arizona State University, right before he moved to Los Angeles. Luke and Brandyn Speckman (right) would later take over the campus work at ASU and eventually lead our church in New York City and oversee all South Asia Churches!

FOR THREE MONTHS, Paul had no results in Ephesus. There is nothing more discouraging than a ministry that is not having many results. The truth is we must have the conviction not to tolerate a lack of fruit. Too many campus leaders are content not to baptize. These ministries begin to look like the youth groups of the world. Charles Spurgeon said, *"I cannot comprehend any one of you Christian people trying to win souls and not having results, being satisfied without results."*[14] Paul was driven and would not keep beating his head against the wall when people were not responding to the gospel.

A passage that has come to mean a lot to me is found in **Isaiah 42:4,** *"He will not falter or be discouraged till He establishes justice on earth. In His teaching the islands will put their hope."* This amazing Messianic prophecy about Jesus says He will not grow discouraged until the world is evangelized! Jesus does not falter or get discouraged. How about you? As campus leaders, we cannot allow disappointment and lack of fruit to get us down. Instead, we need to become even more faithful and solution-oriented during this time. Not being satisfied with a lack of results does not mean we get angry or discouraged. It means we decide to get faithful and innovative. When Paul arrived at Ephesus, he preached for three months, giving his heart, yet Luke does not report much fruit from his efforts. What we do know is that he reaped the backlash of persecution. However, he did not grow discouraged but simply took the disciples to the Lecture Hall of Tyrannus; he changed things up. If you keep doing the same thing expecting different results, that is called insanity. Paul realized his initial "fishing hole" was no longer effective.

---

14 Charles Spurgeon, "Tearful Sowing and Joyful Reaping," *Metropolitan Tabernacle Pulpit* Volume 15, April 25, 1869.

Many years ago, I had just moved to Long Beach, CA, to start a campus ministry at Cal-State Long Beach. At one point, I was growing discouraged as we had not seen a lot of growth. Dr. Kip McKean, my discipler, graciously challenged me that it is always one of two things: Either the students are not working hard enough or are not working smart enough. He encouraged me to go through our campus ministry members and ask them which one they thought it was for them. He based this on **2 Peter 1:8,** *"For if you possess these qualities in increasing measure, they will keep you from being ineffective and unproductive in your knowledge of our Lord Jesus Christ."* The disciples needed to identify why they were ineffective and unproductive. Did they need more teaching and training on working smart, or was God bringing to life the need for repentance in their work ethic for His glory? Encouragingly, as we identified which one it was, our ministry began to see fruit. This region of the church went on to produce some of the most powerful leaders in God's Kingdom. This self-examination is always the place to start when you are leading a dead campus ministry. Is your ministry working hard and not working smart, or are they hardly working?

THE SECRET

Many have called me over the years of doing campus ministry and asked me, "What is the secret? How do we turn our campus ministry around?" Well, I'm finally going to reveal it to everyone… HARD WORK! There is no secret! Truth be told, God has blessed many of my campus ministries with success, but I am not a very social person by nature. I was not a prominent opinion leader in my teen and college days. I am a product of great discipling and imitating those who have gone before me. To this day, I struggle with timidity and talking to strangers. The one thing that has overcome all of that is my work ethic and imitating what works.

In track, I had great success in the Junior Olympics and placed at state. My specialty was the 400-meter hurdles and the 110-meter high hurdles. I was not the fastest runner when it came to just pure speed. My competition was built, strong, and solid. Those who met me would naturally think I was a distance runner based on my tall, lean frame. Let us just say I was not very intimidating in the small tank top and short shorts they make you wear! Many would be surprised at how I could beat those who were faster than me. The secret was focusing on my form over the hurdles. My technique and form were so good, gliding over a hurdle that it cut down my time, allowing me to keep up or beat those faster than me. You do not have to be the most talented, outgoing, or polished person to have an effective campus ministry. Hard work is your hurdle form that will make you "out crank" even the most talented campus minister.

You are probably already doing everything you need to be doing. I am sure you share your faith, study the Bible with people, follow-up with people, rinse, and repeat. Hard work is just multiplying the effort you are currently doing by 100 times! I am not even kidding. You probably just need to do way more of what you are already doing. Discouragement from working hard without results is often Satan's tactic to stop the work of God.

In most cases, I find that this is the reason why ministries are not bearing fruit. Are you bold enough to take an honest inventory of your life right now? How many students are you actually sharing with every week? Be honest with yourself. How many new relationships did you start on campus this past week? *"You reap what you sow,"* is a biblical principle. If you share a lot, you will reap a lot of baptisms. It starts with the campus leader deciding to give himself over to good, old-fashioned hard work.

WORK SMART

Maybe your ministry works really hard, sharing their faith with droves of people, but there are no results. Are tons of people going through the Bible study series only to quit studying and not become a disciple? Of course, it could be a spiritual issue, such as hidden sin. (**Joshua 7**) However, as this handbook examines the practical side of campus ministry, we will look at another possible reason, which, as Kip said, maybe that the students are not working smart. There may need to be teaching on adequate evangelism practicals to turn the ministry around. The practical teachings would include how to share your faith in a way that is relatable to the students, lead Bible studies to move the heart, and discern who is open and, therefore, in whom you should be investing your time.

In **Mark 1:14-20**, when Jesus called the fishermen to follow Him, He struck up a conversation about fishing (even though He was a carpenter). Jesus worked smart! He was relatable in striking up a conversation. Time must be taken to teach your students how to be relatable. Relatability comes through imitation. As a young disciple in the teen ministry, since I was naturally a loner of sorts, I would imitate my football player friend who was a disciple in the church and very fruitful. We can always improve our relatability with non-Christian friends by dressing well and participating in activities popular with students.

As stated earlier, maybe the ministry needs a crash course through First Principles. Condense it to two weeks and have your student leaders meet at your place Monday, Wednesday, and Friday at 10:00 PM and teach them how to do the studies effectively. Sometimes you must equip people in setting up a Bible study. In your campus leader's group, you could practice setting up studies with non-Christians through role-playing. Another skill to teach students is how to share their faith in a cold-contact situation. More on this later.

THE CRAZY FARMER PRINCIPLE

In **Matthew 13**, Jesus used parables to teach His disciples the secrets of the kingdom of God. He says to them, *"Because the knowledge of the secrets of the kingdom of heaven has been given to you..."* (**Matthew 13:11**) He then tells the Parable of the Sower about a farmer who goes out and scatters seeds. Some of the seeds fall on the path, some on rocky places, some on thorny places, and others on good soil. Jesus reveals to us that the seed is the message of the kingdom of God, and each of the four places the seed falls represents the different hearts of men responding to the message. The fact is, not everyone will respond when we bring them the message. Some will be hardhearted like the seed that falls on the path; others will become disciples and quickly fall away like the seed on the rocky soil; some will decide to follow Jesus, but the worries of this life and greed choke out the Word in their life; but praise God, others will become Christians and multiply many disciples! The part that many miss in this parable is the hero of the story...the farmer! What type of farmer throws seed on paths, thorns, rocks, and good soil? Could he not see where he was throwing? Was something wrong with this farmer? A picture emerges of a crazy farmer who just throws seeds everywhere! That is precisely the point; he throws seeds everywhere, no matter what type of soil it is.

As disciples, we cannot see the type of hearts men and women have initially, but we can "throw the seed" onto the soil of every student's heart we encounter! This is the secret of spreading the kingdom's message, being the crazy farmer who is just throwing seeds all over the place. If your disciples practice "the crazy farmer principle," something is bound to grow, and you are going to hit some good soil eventually. Campus ministry in its purest form is sharing your faith with lots and lots and lots of people! That *is* the secret!

One of the most fruitful brothers I have ever known is a brother named Jamal Ellis. He has converted opinion leaders, such as former FOX News anchor Kristin Smith, as well as church leaders and missionaries like Evangelist Coltin Rohn, Women's Ministry Leader Ashley Tambaur, and most importantly to me...my wife Chenelle, who is my favorite Women's Ministry Leader! Some of the highest-profile people in our movement were converted by this man. He would be OK with me sharing this, but to be honest, when I first met him in my campus ministry at ASU, he was kind of a crazy guy. Jamal was not a Bible Talk leader or very eloquent at speaking. Yet everywhere this man went, he shared his faith. He reminds me of the crazy farmer scattering the seed everywhere. He never stopped and was incredibly bold. It made some disciples uncomfortable being with him while he shared his faith. The result, though, was a harvest of leaders. Your campus students need to have new visitors out to your events if you expect to grow. Only by sharing your faith with anyone and everyone will you consistently have new visitors out. Will you decide to imitate the crazy farmer from the parable?

A future Chenelle Patterson (right), who was converted at 19 in the author's campus ministry at Arizona State, is pictured here sporting the campus club's LIFE T-shirts at an evangelism tabling event!

REDEFINING FAITH

Faith must be understood measurably. You can measure the faith of a ministry by its work ethic. **James 2** says faith is seen in what we do. If you believe Jesus is the Savior of the world, you will work hard to bring His message to all people. **Mark 6:5-6** says, *"He could not do any miracles there, except lay His hands on a few sick people and heal them. He was amazed at their lack of faith."* It is surprising and comforting at the same time to know that Jesus had a time when not much was moving in His ministry. Jesus never sinned as He would not allow His ministry to remain in that state indefinitely, but instead, He would turn this dead ministry into a thriving one. Jesus was limited to the faith of the people by God's sovereign choice. In the Scripture mentioned above, we find the biblical principle that where there is no faith, there will be no miracles.

When there are no miracles in the campus ministry, does it amaze you? The Bible is clear that Jesus was amazed at the lack of faith. You must get shocked by it if you are to be like Jesus. Something is not right when our campus ministries are not growing. Jesus did not then blame the people and grow discouraged. He knew faith was the solution! Where there is faith, there will be miracles! Remember, faith is seen in deeds. Yes, all-night prayer nights are vital! Yes, preaching a great sermon is critical! Yes, having all the Christians confess their sins is essential. Yet notice, that Jesus did not do any of those things in this situation. Jesus gets the disciples to work!

> *"Then Jesus went around teaching from village to village. Calling the Twelve to Him, He began to send them out two by two and gave them authority over impure spirits. These were His instructions: "Take nothing for the journey except a staff— no bread, no bag, no money in your belts. Wear sandals but not an extra shirt. Whenever you enter a house, stay there until you leave that town. And if any place will not welcome you or listen to you, leave that place and shake the dust off your feet as a testimony against them." They went out and preached that people should repent. They drove out many demons and anointed many sick people with oil and healed them."*
>
> **-MARK 6:6-13**

> *"The apostles gathered around Jesus and reported to Him all they had done and taught."*
>
> **-MARK 6:30**

PERSONAL EXAMPLE

Before sending the disciples to preach, Jesus Himself starts teaching from village to village. When the ministry is at a standstill, it is important to start sharing your faith yourself. The campus leader must bring visitors to Bible Talk and church. *"Don't let anyone look down on you because you are young, but set an example for the believers in speech, in conduct, in love, in faith and in purity."* (**1 Timothy 4:12**) Leaders must set an example in faith, which means the example will be seen in their deeds. Next, Jesus called the Twelve to Him, calling them to His example. Jesus would not call His disciples to do anything He had not done Himself. He calls them to go out and preach the word as He had already been doing. Before you can turn any ministry around, you have first to be an example in your personal evangelism.

The author's father and mother in the faith—Matt and Helen Sullivan. He will always be grateful to them for taking a loan out on their house to hire him for his first full-time ministry experience as the ASU campus minister. He would later marry the author and his wife and appoint them an Evangelist and Women's Ministry Leader!

ACCOUNTABILITY

Jesus gives the disciples specific instructions, implementing some major accountability to help them. Jesus does not allow them to take any money, food, or an extra shirt. An extra shirt functioned in this time almost as a jacket because the desert would get cold at night in Israel. Hospitality was practiced in this culture to travelers depending on the trust built in the initial encounter. Essentially, Jesus was saying to His disciples that they better find someone open to their message who would allow the disciples into their home to hear the message of the kingdom. Otherwise, they would go hungry that night and be freezing in the wilderness! This may seem extreme to some. I imagine if a campus minister said to his ministry that they could not have any food until they meet someone who takes them out to eat and that is open to studying the Bible, it would probably be controversial. We must understand that Jesus was building a leadership core in the Apostles that would be the foundation for the first-century church. (**Ephesians 2:19-21**) There needed to be intensity in their accountability, and to imitate our Lord, we must implement hardline accountability in our ministries. Even more, accountability is practiced upon the disciple's return. Jesus wants to know what they had done and what was taught. (**Mark 6:30**) The result was 5,000 men, not including the women and children, who came with them! Jesus would miraculously feed the 5,000. Jesus' campaign resulted in over 5,000 visitors!

This type of accountability seems almost too intense to the modern reader. Yet, Jesus understood that all of world evangelism depended on these men. After you start sharing your faith as the leader, you must call your students to your example and send them out to preach. The expectation must be that your students will work just as hard as you do. In sending them out to preach, you must implement accountability. We live in a different culture; taking your disciple's food away and challenging them not to eat until they find an open person may not be the most effective for the campus situation (although fasting until the ministry has a baptism has proven effective)! This is where the "evangelism campaign" comes in handy, which practices the same principles of Jesus!

EVANGELISM CAMPAIGNS

"Campaign" is a term that, as a noun, simply means "a series of military operations intended to achieve a particular objective, confined to a particular area, or involving a specified type of fighting." As a verb, it means "work in an organized and active way toward a particular goal, typically a political or social one." The "evangelism campaign" is an operation geared at generating more visitors and Bible studies for the harvest of souls in the campus ministry. **1 Samuel 18:16** says, *"But all Israel and Judah loved David, because he led them in their campaigns."* Israel was drawn to David because he led the people in their campaigns. A successful campaign builds loyalty in your ministry.

Before planning your evangelism campaign, you must know the difference between *faith goals* and *effort goals.* The secular world understands this, using the terms performance versus achievement goals. A good salesman will have a goal to make a certain number of sales in a given day (faith goal). He must believe he can hit that goal, but he can only control the number of phone calls he makes or doors on which he knocks in his attempt to sell his product (effort goal). Both types of goals are necessary to achieve great success. *Faith goals* are what we desire to happen but ultimately have no control over. For example, I could challenge my campus ministry to set up two new Bible studies every day this week. The truth is that this is entirely out of their control. They could share their faith with every single unopen person that day! If your campaign is based solely on faith goals, it can do untold damage to your people's faith since the truth is, they are not in control of those results—God is. This is because Biblical faith is always accompanied by effort, or as James would say deeds. **(James 2:14-26)**

Think of effort goals as ones we can control. For example, I can tell my ministry to share their faith with five people every day this week. Regardless of the non-Christians' response to their sharing, they are in total control of sharing with five people. The point is that this is something everyone can do and achieve success. The disciples feeling victorious is crucial to the morale and even the faith of the ministry. To have a campaign with the goal of everyone bringing a visitor to Bible Talk is in the faith goal realm and not in your control. To have a campaign in which everyone must pray for an hour a day is in the effort goal realm since that is in their control. The effort exhorted shows their faith in God. Both faith goals and effort goals work together to produce miraculous results. If you only encourage people to set effort goals and do not inspire Christians to have faith goals, your campaign relies too heavily on human strength. Faith and effort goals complement each other, just as James argues, *"You see that his [Abraham's] faith and his actions were working together, and his faith was made complete by what he did."* **(James 2:22)** In the following section, I will show how to include special *stipulations* in your evangelism campaign that will maximize its effectiveness.

THE LIFE CAMPAIGN

Let me share an example of one of the most successful campaigns we have seen God bless. First, you want to come up with a theme for the campaign. You could base it on **John 10:10,** where Jesus says, "I have come that they may have life, and have it to the full." If Jesus came to bring life to the full, then perhaps you can call your evangelism strategy, *The LIFE Campaign!*" The Friday Campus devotional before the week you are doing the campaign, you want to preach an inspiring sermon that introduces the theme and campaign to the campus ministry. This sermon should be visionary and passionate. In my first campus ministry at ASU, I borrowed a theme I heard growing up called *The LIFE Campaign.* LIFE was an acronym that stood for *"Love is for Everyone."* We wanted everyone's heart in the right place for the lost before we rolled out the campaign. You might also do a "Jericho March" around the campus, praying for God to give you the land. **(Joshua 1 & 6)** After your lesson, you want to pass out a sheet that has all the disciples paired up with a partner every day for that week (Monday-Friday). When you prepare this beforehand, it is crucial to put a more experienced or effective disciple with a newer or more timid disciple setting up the entire ministry to be successful. Many have killed their ministries' faith with campaigns because they did not prepare it to be successful by thinking through each student and who they will be paired up with. Preparing this sheet is crucial. This sheet also includes the daily sharing number goal for the campaign, important meetings during campaign week (prayer times), stipulations of the campaign, and how to report your numbers. Remember, Jesus was focused on the details when sending the seventy out two by two, and we need to be as well. **(Luke 10)** I believe it is the specific direction and details that give the disciples security in evangelism campaigns, both in Jesus' time and today. Every disciple then knows with whom they are sharing, the daily expectations, and how to report the numbers for each day of the campaign week. They are also equipped for the task.

Your campaign then needs an effort goal that is attainable but challenging for your ministry. A good number is to challenge your campus ministry to share their faith with 50 people a day for that week. As the leader, you then tell them you are going to share with 100 people a day. That is the effort goal that everyone can attain and is being held accountable to. You can also throw in some "stipulations" to motivate everyone to be effective and not just hand out invitations. For example, if they are in a personal Bible study that day with a non-Christian, that can count for "ten" in your campaign. So, if you were in five Bible studies, you are already done with your campaign for the day. Getting a phone number from a non-Christian interested in coming out to one of your events could count as "five" of your campaign number goal. These stipulations make the higher number of effort goals more bearable and achievable while also producing the results you want: contact numbers and Bible studies. Saturday can be a fun night to end the campaign, where the disciples gather for fellowship and food while following up by calling and texting the contacts they met during the campaign about coming to church the next morning and while praying for God to open their hearts. Other parts to the campaign you can include are 6:00 AM prayer times, a daily Bible Talk hosted by you at a high population center on campus, etc. You want to provide multiple opportunities for the thousands with whom will be shared to come to hear the message. The essential question is: How does the campus leader hold people accountable in these campaigns?

CAMPAIGN ACCOUNTABILITY

There are different things you can do. When our ministry at the University of Central Florida was small and in its infancy (around seven disciples), we had them come to meet at the brothers' apartment at 10:00 PM and share the good news about how it went for the day. This time of sharing inspired all who were present to see God working! I remember one brother sharing with over a 100 himself! He had never done anything like this and had so much fun sharing his faith. You can also do accountability by having everyone text you how many people they shared with that day. You can then put together a mass text that has everyone's name on it and includes how many each person shared with that day. It can be encouraging to see the hundreds that were reached in one day and identify disciples who may need help meeting their goals. Another successful form of accountability is to have the disciples text you the names of the people committed for service Sunday (or whatever event your campaign is building up for). This mode of accountability helps put a name to someone to pray for them and focuses more on people who are committed to coming. Depending on your ministry's size, you may need to work through your Bible Talk leaders to regulate a successful system of accountability if you cannot personally follow up with everyone. The evangelism campaign is crucial to turning any dead campus ministry around. What about the disciples who do not participate or refuse to take part in the campaign?

DEALING WITH THE UNCOMMITTED, TIMID, AND WEAK

Different campus ministers have talked to me about handling the students in their ministry who do not participate in the campaign. Every situation is a case-by-case situation. Indeed, there is no "one size fits all" approach to ministry, but the Bible gives us clear directives on dealing with certain types of issues in the ministry. We must be sure to prescribe the right "medicine" to the proper "sickness." **1 Thessalonians 5:14** says, *"And we urge you, brothers and sisters, warn those who are idle and disruptive, encourage the disheartened, help the weak, be patient with everyone."* The Bible is clear that the idle disciple needs to be warned. Idle can mean the lazy disciple, but the word idle also means, in the original language, to be "out of rank" or, as the NIV adds, "disruptive." This person is rebellious and needs to be rebuked because their heart is hardened, as they are not in step with the spirit of the ministry's campaign. A rebuke may seem extreme, but with idleness or rebellion towards the direction of leadership, there is always a heart issue. Someone might say, "Where are evangelism campaigns in the Bible?" "Is it a sin for me to not share with the number you gave me for this campaign?" As Jesus did many times, you may respond to a question like that with a question. "Why would you not want to share with 50 people a day?" Asking questions draws out the heart to find out if it is genuinely uncommitted or needs help finding a way to be obedient. Maybe some students do not see a way to share with that many amid their schedules. In some rare cases, they might not be able to share with that many. That is where you, as their leader, must really be aware of all the disciple's situations and maybe adjust things personally for them. They are not idle if their schedule is too packed to do a high number goal campaign. If this is the case, maybe ask them what number goal they think they could achieve, personalizing the campaign for them. Never lose sight of what the goal is, spreading the message of Christ to other students. It does not help to be legalistically stuck to your campaign system if one of your disciples is drowning in anxiety and overwhelmed. From my experience, most are not rebellious but just need faith, help, and encouragement.

The disheartened or timid disciple needs encouragement. It may be that you need to go with them specifically and do the campaign with them. They need to know that God is with them and that you believe in them. This Christian is not uncommitted; they are simply scared to share their faith. I have found when I go out with disciples like this and share my faith with them; they get so fired up. They have a chance to watch me do it and a model to imitate.

Lastly, Paul said we need to help the weak disciple. Some students have a course load of classes that make them weak. Be sensitive and do not get so stuck on the campaign's number goal that you lose discernment or compassion. Be willing to change things for specific situations, as stated earlier. When the students feel considered by your leadership, they will be grateful and loyal. We can be too quick to label someone as "out of rank" or rebellious instead of realizing they need help in their schedule or life. Finally, be patient with everyone. I do not get too caught up with those "who aren't really with us" in the campaigns. Too many leaders get focused on the few "bad apples" instead of focusing on those with good hearts. Focus on the disciples who want to make a difference, and in time, the others will either repent or eventually leave. Let it never be said, though, that we did not do everything we could to help our students be successful in their evangelistic campaigns!

BUILD A SOLD-OUT BASE OF DISCIPLES

Campaigns help make your ministry sold out and build a solid base. In **1 Corinthians 3:5-13**, Paul tells the church in Corinth that he built congregations as an expert builder. He lets us know the foundation is Jesus Christ, and that how one builds will be shown when the fires of trials come on the ministry. The key is the foundation! The foundation being Christ means that every disciple in your campus ministry must be called to be just like Jesus. Before I even introduce a campaign, there have been many times that I will have an evening of renewal and recommitment to the covenant we made with God at baptism. The covenant renewal will usually include a lesson on being open with sin and, afterward, discipling groups with confession. Often, you just must get all the sin out of the ministry, and then the people will be ready for an evangelistic crusade! Sin always steals faith and confidence before God. Remember **Psalm 127:1,** *"Unless the LORD builds the house, the builders labor in vain."* The ministry must be with God.

When Paul's ministry hit a standstill for three months, he had to go campaign with his twelve disciples, who were his first converts in Ephesus, (**Acts 19:1-5**) and call them to be with him every day to have discussions on the campus. It was this evangelistic campaign that started a revolution that evangelized Asia in two years! Suppose you have been hitting a wall for the last couple of months. In that case, it is time to imitate the faith of Jesus and Paul by starting to preach the gospel yourself, call your people to do the same, and organize an effective campaign to facilitate this preaching. Expect people to work as hard as you do. Of course, with all the sharing and new Bible studies, new obstacles will come that must be overcome.

CHAPTER 6

ARGUING PERSUASIVELY—
BECOMING A SOUL WINNER

THERE IS NO DOUBT that Paul believed we must be effective and persuasive when sharing our faith. Consider the following two scriptures:

> *"At Iconium Paul and Barnabas went as usual into the Jewish synagogue. There they spoke so effectively that a great number of Jews and Greeks believed."*
>
> **-ACTS 14:1**

> *"Since, then, we know what it is to fear the Lord, we try to persuade others. What we are is plain to God, and I hope it is also plain to your conscience."*
>
> **-2 CORINTHIANS 5:11**

Richie and Elizabeth McDonell, with whom the author and his wife had the privilege of studying the Bible. They are true partners in the gospel and have done campus ministry at UCLA in the past and are currently leading the great Minneapolis-St. Paul International Christian Church.

Arguing persuasively does not always guarantee results, as seen in the last chapter when Paul had to move to his campus—the Lecture Hall of Tyrannus. However, it is evident from these passages that his speaking ability and passion for persuading brought more souls into the kingdom. It has been said that knowledge is power. This principle rings true throughout Scripture, as knowledge allows us to be persuasive. **Hosea 4:6** shows the converse to be true, *"...my people are destroyed for lack of knowledge."* A campus ministry that is not well-versed in the Bible will be destroyed.

GO DEEP

In **Ezekiel 47:1-12,** Ezekiel is shown a vision of a great temple that foreshadows God's church.

The man brought me back to the entrance to the temple, and I saw water coming out from under the threshold of the temple toward the east (for the temple faced east). The water was coming down from under the south side of the temple, south of the altar. He then brought me out through the north gate and led me around the outside to the outer gate facing east, and the water was trickling from the south side.

As the man went eastward with a measuring line in his hand, he measured off a thousand cubits and then led me through water that was ankle-deep. He measured off another thousand cubits and led me through water that was knee-deep. He measured off another thousand and led me through water that was up to the waist. He measured off another thousand, but now it was a river that I could not cross, because the water had risen and was deep enough to swim in—a river that no one could cross. He asked me, "Son of man, do you see this?"

Then he led me back to the bank of the river. When I arrived there, I saw a great number of trees on each side of the river. He said to me, "This water flows toward the eastern region and goes down into the Arabah, where it enters the Dead Sea. When it empties into the sea, the salty water there becomes fresh. Swarms of living creatures will live wherever the river flows. There will be large numbers of fish, because this water flows there and makes the salt water fresh; so where the river flows everything will live. Fishermen will stand along the shore; from En Gedi to En Eglaim there will be places for spreading nets. The fish will be of many kinds—like the fish of the Mediterranean Sea. But the swamps and marshes will not become fresh; they will be left for salt. Fruit trees of all kinds will grow on both banks of the river. Their leaves will not wither, nor will their fruit fail. Every month they will bear fruit, because the water from the sanctuary flows to them. Their fruit will serve for food and their leaves for healing."

Water comes bubbling up from under the altar and eventually forms a mighty river that makes life appear even in the Dead Sea! This water represents the Holy Spirit which first comes under the altar, which is where sacrifices were made, showing us the Holy Spirit would come only by sacrifice, looking forward to the sacrifice of Christ. After the sacrifice of Christ, the Holy Spirit was poured out to the disciples who became that mighty river who evangelized the nations in their generation!

The angel measures different levels of the water and correspond-ing Spirit, revealing to us the different levels of commitment the people of God can have in their relationship with their Creator. As Christians, this represents our level of discipleship following Jesus. The first is **ankle-deep.** If you have ever stood in ankle-deep water, it is effortless to step out. Christians that are ankle-deep in the Word of God are not committed to the kingdom of God and Jesus and will quickly step out. Every new disciple is at this level and must be attended to daily. **Knee-deep** water represents prayer and dependence on God. Christians that are knee-deep tend to pray when things are going hard, but again, there are back doors open to leave God's Kingdom still. **Waste-deep** is where most Christians are at. We are in the water, walking around and enjoying the refreshment that comes from doing so, but we are still tempted to be in control of our lives, choosing how deep we will go.

In looking for treasure, the real treasures in the seas and oceans are always found on the seafloor. So, it is the same with God's Word. Ezekiel finally reveals where God intends us to be—in a **mighty river** where all the fishermen (disciples) are out catching the big fish! To catch the "big fish" on campus, your ministry must go deep into the Spirit of our God. Do you want to convert the fraternity guy or sorority girl? The quarterback on the football team? Would you like to convert the president of a political activist group on campus? You must be "all in" when it comes to the Scriptures and the Holy Spirit. I picture white water rafting where the rapids just take you, and the people in the boat are totally out of control! God desires we are so deep in His Word that His Spirit can only take us where He wants us to go![15]

Having been on college campuses such as Harvard and Columbia University, I understand the importance of knowing the Bible at a deep level. Many would not have been converted if anyone else in my ministry was studying with them. Saying this is not an arrogant

---

15 For deeper study, please see Dr. Kip McKean's upcoming book containing all the sermons from the ICCM Bachelor's program, including the "River of God" sermon, based on Ezekiel 47.

statement; it is just the truth. Because of the calling of the Holy Spirit through the discipling of godly men, I did put in the effort, the years of studying God's Word at a deeper level. Therefore, I was the only one who could answer their questions to deal with their hearts using the right approach that was needed. Now I am calling my "Timothys" to do the same so we can flood the most influential campuses in Boston with fully equipped leaders. God promises to give wisdom to those who will humbly ask Him. **(James 1:5)** Many ask for wisdom because of **James 1:5,** but we cannot forget **James 2:** Faith without deeds is useless. If faith requires deeds, it means you cannot ask God for something you are not going to put in the effort to get. Do you have a plan to work daily at plumbing the depths of the Word of God to find the treasures just waiting for you in your Bible? **(Proverbs 2:1-8)**

Fang Ha was met in Boston by the disciples during a public
preaching event. She now serves the ministry with
her husband, in Sydney Australia.

THEOLOGY

When I lived in Gainesville, FL, in the "Bible Belt," there were hundreds of churches within that tiny city. I have done teachings for our campus ministry on what these various churches believe. We have studied Calvinism, different denominations, pre-millennialism, spiritual warfare, Pentecostalism, the Sabbath, faith and works, and much more. This knowledge of theology produced a group of leaders who can effectively swing the sword of God's Word in their evangelism and studies with many different types of people. However, there are some Christians who can exhibit an anti-intellectual bias. These dear brothers and sisters may chuckle and even mock the idea of studying theology and doctrine, saying things like, "I'm just going to stay focused on making disciples," implying that I am wasting my time studying the Scriptures to this depth. The fact is they lack depth and the ability to make disciples of the religious and intellectuals. It is easy to blow off someone as "not open" when the truth is you did not have the knowledge or skill to convert them. The result is a ministry unable to bring in the big fish, the future Paul's waiting to be convinced, if you only convert those who are "easy" to convert.

It has been encouraging for me to see youth leaders, students in "Christian" fraternities, and religious people become disciples over the years. I went to a four-year Bible college, getting my bachelor's degree in biblical studies. It was terrific to convert two people on the track team and another on the soccer team. Though it was a religious school, people were open! My study life has always been strong. The campus leader must have a study life in which they are continually learning and taking time at least once every two months to have a devotional or a discipleship group focused on in-depth biblical teachings. You must equip the saints for works of service.

I find that a ministry that has this element learns to think critically and logically so they know how and when to use the Scriptures. The campus minister can take shortcuts by simply telling the students what to do in every situation, and this will work to some extent. If you teach your students to think critically and logically about faith, they will think on their feet and adapt to various situations. In turn, it will help them become more effective at presenting a Bible study to their friends or inviting them to church.

RELATIONAL EVANGELISM

Another incredible opportunity for evangelism will come from the relationships the students already have. If you build the entire ministry depending on growth from your campaigns and cold-contact evangelism, you will become a campaign-only-driven ministry. To be clear, campaigns are awesome and much needed, especially to jump-start a ministry at the beginning of the term. A campus evangelism campaign is typically a week or two-week "blitz" or push to have your group share their faith with large numbers of people, usually accompanied by number goals and daily accountability. Campaign-only-driven ministries tend to create a feeling that ministry is a grind and a duty.

Since ministries that are campaign-heavy can lead to burnout, you must encourage students to continue to build relationships with people. Students need to be reminded of the massive opportunity within their relationships in their classes, with their roommates, and within their chosen college-sponsored activities and orga-nizations. It teaches them not just to share their faith only 30 or so minutes before Bible Talk begins but also with the multitudes of people they are around daily. Visitors have often come out to service because of a simple encouragement to my ministry to text message all the numbers they already have on their phones! Try it today. If everyone does it, I guarantee someone will come out just from that. The leader must remind the students that they are always around people every day. You must encourage them to not sit in the same seat or section of class every time, but to sit near new people with whom they can potentially share the gospel. The fact they are in the same class makes it "relational" and more nat-ural. Students continuously have people "cold-contacting" them to join clubs, sign petitions, join religious groups, and the list goes on. Relational evangelism does not take as many skills of persuasion. A situation such as being in the same class, dorm, or sports team has already cultivated the soil for a relationship to form. The sheer fact they share something in common can establish the friendship. On the other hand, cold-contact evangelism truly takes being prepared to answer on the spot. (**1 Peter 3:15**)

Let's avoid either extreme by focusing only on one form of evan-gelism or the other (**Ecclesiastes 7:18**) and be like Jesus who prac-ticed both. By using the tools we spoke about in this chapter, you will equip your campus disciples to argue persuasively and win many souls.

CHAPTER 7

ARGUING PERSUASIVELY PART 2— OVERCOMING OBJECTIONS

OCCASIONALLY, as I am preaching, I will ask everyone to raise their hand who has become a Christian through someone randomly inviting them "cold contact." It always impresses the church, as half or more of the room has their hand up! We cannot underestimate the power of cold-contact evangelism. With the Samaritan woman at the well, we see a great example of cold-contact evangelism, but then the woman went and brought the whole town—this is relational evangelism! **(John 4:7-42)** Jesus's ministry had both and so must ours.

"I'm not religious." "I don't have the time." "I'm not interested, thank you." Anyone who has spent time in campus ministry is familiar with these responses when cold-contact sharing and even in sharing with our friends. How do we respond to these responses in our cold-contact evangelism? Let us go to a passage that has helped guide me in sharing my faith over the years, understanding people, and determining what God's will is for me and my hearers. Ezekiel had been overwhelmed for seven days, and finally, the Spirit comes into him, and he is told to stand up and do something:

> *He said: "Son of man, I am sending you to the Israelites, to a rebellious nation that has rebelled against me; they and their ancestors have been in revolt against me to this very day. The people to whom I am sending you are obstinate and stubborn. Say to them, 'This is what the Sovereign Lord says.' And whether they listen or fail to listen—for they are a rebellious people—they will know that a prophet has been among them. And you, son of man, do not be afraid of them or their words. Do not be afraid, though briers and thorns are all around you and you live among scorpions. Do not be afraid of what they say or be terrified by them, though they are a rebellious people. You must speak my words to them, whether they listen or fail to listen, for they are rebellious. But you, son of man, listen to what I say to you. Do not rebel like that rebellious people; open your mouth and eat what I give you."*
>
> **-EZEKIEL 2: 3-8**

God did not send Ezekiel to the most open group of people! They were obstinate, stubborn, and downright selfish. God tells Ezekiel to preach so that the people will know that a prophet has been among them (**Ezekiel 2:5**)! We must understand that the people we are being sent to are obstinate, stubborn, and selfish. They are on their way to class, to leave campus, to an appointment, to do homework, etc., and when you, a random stranger, interrupt what they are doing, most could care less about what you have to say. It helps to put yourself in their shoes. How do you respond if a random person approaches you about something? What grabs your attention and what repels you? They are resolved in their selfish desires of the day. They did not wake up, in most cases, hoping someone would invite them to church. What is the man or woman of God to do? Make sure they know a prophet has been among them! You are reading this book right now. How would you feel if someone interrupted you to talk about something? If you read on, God offers Ezekiel something to eat, His very words:

And He said to me, "Son of man, eat what is before you, eat this scroll; then go and speak to the people of Israel." So I opened my mouth, and He gave me the scroll to eat. Then He said to me, "Son of man, eat this scroll I am giving you and fill your stomach with it." So I ate it, and it tasted as sweet as honey in my mouth. He then said to me: "Son of man, go now to the people of Israel and speak my words to them. You are not being sent to a people of obscure speech and strange language, but to the people of Israel—not to many peoples of obscure speech and strange language, whose words you cannot understand. Surely if I had sent you to them, they would have listened to you. But the people of Israel are not willing to listen to you because they are not willing to listen to me, for all the Israelites are hardened and obstinate. But I will make you as unyielding and hardened as they are. I will make your forehead like the hardest stone, harder than flint. Do not be afraid of them or terrified by them, though they are a rebellious people."

-EZEKIEL 3:1-9

God has Ezekiel eat His words before going out, and it tasted as sweet as honey. (**Ezekiel 3:3; Psalm 19:10**) Now he is filled with God's Word, but the people are still unyielding and hardened; this is the state of many people in our colleges around the world. God has a plan to change things. He is going to make the modern-day Ezekiels (all our campus brothers and sisters) as unyielding and hardened as their opponents are! He is going to make their foreheads harder than flint! Flint was the hardest-known stone at the time. The idea here is that God will make Ezekiel's resolve and conviction to preach more intense than their resolve to be selfish; this is what it takes! You must understand that God, through His Spirit, has given you the ability to be more passionate than others are selfish. You must have more conviction to be zealous in winning them to Christ than they do to be selfish. You must have the conviction to share your faith in such a way that they will know a prophet has been among them.

Do you share in a way that, regardless of their response, they will never forget about you? Your resolve for them being saved must outweigh their determination to get to where they were heading before you shared with them! Do you share your faith in such a way that the people will never forget it? Of course, this does not mean being outlandish, but using tact and getting to the heart.

DESTROYING STRONGHOLDS

Too often, at the first excuse or reason they give us as to why they cannot come to church or Bible Talk, we give up and move on. We need to be the ones with the foreheads of flint, hammering our way through the different barriers of excuses and reasons they give.

Remember, the bigger the fish, the harder it is to reel up on the fishing line. The principle applies to getting people to church. The "bigger fish," the more of an opinion leader they are, the harder it will be to "catch" them. I call these barriers or excuses non-Christians give while evangelizing "strongholds." Satan is called the "strong man" in the Bible, and he holds unbelievers captive by creating strongholds of the mind.

> "The weapons we fight with are not the weapons of the world. On the contrary, they have divine power to demolish strongholds. We demolish arguments and every pretension that sets itself up against the knowledge of God, and we take captive every thought to make it obedient to Christ."
> **-2 CORINTHIANS 10:4-5**

A stronghold is also a fortress that protects the city from an incoming invasion. The army attempts to block an incoming attack from out of the stronghold. For this reason, I will call the initial deflections that people give you when sharing your faith "blocks." The Spirit reveals here that Satan can set up strongholds of the mind. These are strong thinking patterns ingrained in the mind that take divine power from God's Word to change. God's people demolish these arguments that set themselves up against the truth. We can take captive the thoughts other people have, using the Bible to bring them to a knowledge of the truth. How do we destroy some of the initial strongholds that prevent people from coming out to your campus event or church?

Jesus said it takes one or two witnesses to validate an official church decision in resolving conflict based on the Old Testament's judicial system. (**Matthew 18:15-20; Deuteronomy 19:15**) According to Jesus, after a brother or sister who committed the offense is confronted three times (by the offender, two or three witnesses, and then the church) and are still unrepentant, they are to be treated as a pagan or tax collector. There is something to the idea of two or three times. Even in **Titus 3:10,** a divisive person is warned only twice and then excommunicated. The testimony of two or three (whether witnesses or times warned) is significant to God, and after two or three times, you can be sure the person has chosen not to respond on a heart-level. Taking this principle, I find it to be a useful guide, even in sharing with non-Christians, to determine the openness of one's heart. I believe you should attempt to overcome each "block" (we are calling blocks responses such as "I'm not religious," "I go to church already," "I'm too busy," etc.) three times, and if they are still not responsive, it is time to *"shake the dust off your feet"* and move on. (**Matthew 10:14**) What are some of these blocks we must overcome on campus? Let us look at some of these common reasons or excuses and fight our way through them.

Before getting into how you can respond to these, a fundamental conviction we find from Jesus in dealing with people is to respond to a question with a question. Jesus asked 307 questions in the gospels, and out of the 183 questions that people asked Him, He answered only three. Observing the questions Jesus asked gives us insight into the evangelistic method of Jesus Christ ... asking questions! If someone says, "I already go to church," do not end the conversation, ask them, "What church do you go to?" or "How long have you been going there?" The goal of any cold contact is to connect, and questions are the pathway to connection. It is not so much as saying the "right" thing but making that connection with them. Making a connection is done if you can keep the person talking. My go-to when I do not know what to say is to keep asking questions. Questions draw a person's heart out while bringing their guard down. Most people love talking about themselves, and if you can remember this principle, most of what follows here will come naturally. If you forget everything in this section, just remember, keep asking questions and you will still find success in your cold-contact evangelism. First, we will look at how to win those who profess to be "Christians."

THE RELIGIOUS

Those who profess to be Christians commonly reply, "I already attend a church" or "I am all set." These responses take many disciples off guard, as the flesh will tell them to respond, "Great, have a nice day." My philosophy toward those who claim to be "Christians" is to treat them as Christian. You know where they stand in your heart before God, but it will naturally challenge them if you treat them as a Christian. You could say, "That is great, you believe in Christ also, could we get together sometime and do a Bible study and exchange testimonies?" An even better response would be, "That is awesome that you believe in Christ; how do you witness (religious world term for sharing your faith) on campus? Could we go together sometime?" The goal is for them to be humbled by your evangelism, testimony, and life. You want to establish yourself as the religious person's discipler or spiritual mentor. Sometimes it is useful to ask them, "Who is discipling you?" They may ask what you mean by that, which then opens up an excellent opportunity to do a discipleship study. Another response if they already have a church is, "That is great! We host a Bible Talk on campus that students from different kinds of churches come to! Could you make that instead?"

Jesus is the ultimate example of how to share our faith with the religious. We forget that all of Jesus' original followers came from the religious background of Judaism. It would shock many Christians to know that Jesus' disciples were not even sure about Him being the Messiah until after following Him for a while! Jesus did not approach the men fishing and ask, "Do you believe I am the Messiah? Have you repented of all your sin? What are your thoughts on baptism? etc." He invited them to follow Him, walk with Him, build a friendship, and knew he would *"make them into fishers of men."* **(Mark 1:16-17)**

College students now more than ever value sincerity, community, and love. We sometimes have this approach that they can only join "our club" if they agree to everything first. We make them feel like they are on the outside until they are baptized. Biblically, we know they are not a Christian until they have declared their faith and been baptized into Christ, but what if we invited them into our lives first and treated them as disciples? Would not this naturally cause them to "live into" being made a disciple? They would naturally become a part of the group, being convicted by the light of true disciples. Studying the Bible for them will be a breeze since there is a relationship already established. I love giving people vision, and I have told them I need them to be a part of our church to lead a specific ministry even before they get baptized. I have allowed those who can sing to participate in the pre-service singing practice. Although only disciples can lead in the worship service, we need to make the religious feel part of the group, giving them a vision for what they can add to our ministries. They then will be receptive to the truth about discipleship and following Jesus.

THE NON-RELIGIOUS

The opposite type of response you can receive from someone on campus is, "I'm not religious." Another version of this is, "I'm not into organized religion." If you are like my friend, Dr. Andrew Smellie, you could reply, "Are you into disorganized religion?" Sometimes this funny response breaks down a barrier and leads to more conversation, but there is the risk of coming off offensive, so trust the Spirit to guide you. You must pray to read people's spirits as you talk to them to gauge the appropriate response. I believe the more we become like Jesus, the more we can be in tune with men's spirits.

Remember, with cold-contact sharing, you are trying to build bridges and connect with people. A simple response to "I'm not religious" is to ask another question. For example, "What is being religious to you?" Most students on campus want to talk and discuss these types of issues. Many, including myself, have responded, "That is great; I'm not religious either. We have a relationship with God, not a religion." However, over time, I have come to find this to be misleading, as the Bible is clear that Christians do have a religion. (**1 Timothy 5:4; James 1:27**) As disciples, we do many religious things, but by asking what they mean by religion, you will find that most people view it as holding to a moral code to find happiness, and they do not see a need for that in their life. It helps to share with the person that true religion is the by-product of a relationship with God. Continue to engage them in conversation after they define religion by probing them about their relationship with God. You could say, "You may enjoy these Thursday evening Bible discussions we have on faith and religion on campus. It is not a formal church service or anything, but just a bunch of students coming together and discussing topics like we are discussing now. I love your thoughts, could I get your number and have you as my guest this Thursday?"

NOT INTERESTED

Perhaps one of the most challenging blocks to overcome is when they say, "I'm not interested." Always remember the principle; responding to a question with a question when you do not know what to say initially. I usually respond to this block by saying, "Could I ask what makes you not interested in it?" The goal is always to keep them talking and generating conversation. Suppose your campus ministry has other events outside of Bible Talk, church, and devotional, such as a basketball league, volleyball night, ultimate frisbee, fitness ministry, open mic nights, etc. In that case, you could invite them to one of these events instead. "I'm not interested" is usually the block given when they just want to get on their way and usually have not even given you the chance to share what you are offering. A similar reply to your cold-contact sharing is, "I'm too busy." A direct and sometimes convicting approach can be to reply, "You are too busy for God?" You can be confrontational and still be loving in your tone. If they claim a belief in God, do not be afraid to use Scripture to challenge them on their priorities. We must be bold and not scared to ask invasive questions that challenge the heart. Jesus did it!

NO FAITH IN JESUS

What about those who come from Muslim, Hindu, or Jewish backgrounds? How about those who claim to be an atheist? It is essential to realize that, according to the Bible, there is no true atheist. God has put eternity into the hearts of mankind. (**Ecclesiastes 3:11**) The apostle Paul teaches through the Holy Spirit that God's Word has been written on the hearts of all mankind. (**Romans 2:15**) Over time, their conscience that was once sensitive to the things of God has now started to defend their sinful actions. **Psalm 14** reveals atheism's true cause; God says they are fools.

Sin is always the root of such claims, and since sin is deceitful, they believe they do not believe in God. (**Hebrews 3:12-13**) Do not allow the smokescreen of "atheism" to take you away from challenging them on their lifestyle. I have found that although apologetics can be helpful, converting an atheist takes challenging them to live as a disciple. **John 7:16-17** says, *"Jesus answered, "My teaching is not my own. It comes from the one who sent me. Anyone who chooses to do the will of God will find out whether my teaching comes from God or whether I speak on my own."* The way someone finds out the truth about Jesus' teaching is by practicing it. Christianity is not so much an intellectual pursuit as much as it is a moral pursuit. Atheists need to come to church events and outings with disciples. If they will not come to a church event, bring your atheist friend with you when the disciples go out to eat, play sports, etc. **John 13:34-35** says, *"A new command I give you: Love one another. As I have loved you, so you must love one another. By this everyone will know that you are my disciples, if you love one another."* They will know we are disciples by our love, not by our knowledge, apologetics, or intellectual arguments. My personal opinion is that apologetics does more to help build the disciples' faith than they do to build the faith of non-Christians. Love is the ultimate conversion tool. The same could be said for Muslims, Hindus, Jews, and any other religion. It is not enough just to get into refuting the beliefs of atheists and world religions; we must get to the heart of the matter. What matters most to God is their hearts.

GETTING TO THE ROOT

Proverbs 19:22 says, "*What a person desires is unfailing love.*" I will never forget Dr. Raul Moreno (who currently oversees some of the fastest growing campus ministries in the SoldOut Movement) teaching a lesson on this verse at a leader's meeting in LA. He made the point that doctrine and truth do not convert people; love converts them. A mind explosion went off for me, as Raul had always tried to help me have more fun in the ministry. Doctrine and truth are necessary to be saved, but what man truly desires is unfailing love, which only God can give. This love is expressed in the body of Christ, the church. You will notice throughout the gospels, Jesus always invited men into His life:

> "When the two disciples heard Him say this, they followed Jesus. Turning around, Jesus saw them following and asked, "What do you want?" They said, "Rabbi" (which means "Teacher"), "where are you staying?" "Come," He replied, "and you will see." So they went and saw where He was staying, and they spent that day with Him. It was about four in the afternoon. Andrew, Simon Peter's brother, was one of the two who heard what John had said and who had followed Jesus. The first thing Andrew did was to find his brother Simon and tell him, "We have found the Messiah" (that is, the Christ). And he brought him to Jesus."
>
> **-JOHN 1:37-42**

Jesus told His first followers they had to come, and they would see. He then proceeded to spend the entire day with them. Jesus so impacted Andrew that he invited his brother to come and see as well. In our terminology, Peter was brought out to the church by a visitor, his brother! **(John 1:40-42)** People got converted by spending time with Jesus, which happens today by spending time with the church, which is the body of Christ. When talking about cold-contact evangelism, the whole goal is to get them around the body of Christ. When they find it, they will bring their friends and family.

Many feel the desire to proclaim the whole counsel of God to someone on first meeting them. I cannot tell you how many students in my ministries always approach me, "Mike, I have this Muslim guy I met on campus. Can you come to do a study with them?" As if I have some secret Scriptures that will immediately show them the error of their way, they will fall proclaiming that Jesus is Lord. I am okay being in those studies, but they will be let down when they see I do not come with some theological treatise on why the Christian faith is valid as a means to convert them. It is love that does it. The person agreeing to study must be willing to study the Bible, read through the Book of John, and build sincere relationships with God and people.

Students should not engage in debates about baptism on first meeting someone. The baptism debate can burn down a bridge before there is even a connection made. Jesus just said, *"Come follow me and I will make you fishers of men."* **(Mark 1:16)** He invited men to walk with Him. You need to remove the pressure that you must convince the atheist of God's existence, that you must persuade the Muslim of Jesus being God, that you must persuade the Baptist that baptism is necessary for salvation, etc., all in one encounter. Throw that thinking out the door! How many have become disciples by doing that? Then why would you continue to do that? Do you really think a religious person has never read **Acts 2:38** or **Matthew 28:18-20**? You will get to that point, but first, there needs to be a discipling relationship established with the person where they know you love them, trust is built, and they see you as their spiritual mentor. Instead of drilling doctrine into them at the beginning, invite them into your life. Build a friendship and let the power of the love in the church do the work as you study the Bible with them. My rule of thumb is unless someone has started coming to church, I am not quick to jump into those Bible studies. Something is wrong if they are on the Cross study and have never been to church. There are always rare exceptions where something must be said at the right moment about seeking out the fellowship, but for the most part, by imitating Jesus, we will see incredible results on our campuses when we love the people with whom we are studying the Bible.

THE SURVEY

I remember being a campus minister at ASU (Arizona State University) and thinking there must be a way to make cold-contact evangelism easier. In truth, this was to help both me and my ministry overcome timidity. Many young disciples live in their timidity and are therefore in**timid**ated to share their faith; others are shy by nature. When I studied the Bible to become a Christian, this was a massive cost for me personally. By nature, I am timid. Although I had friends from different groups, I was never the life of the party, nor did I have a naturally charismatic personality.

One of the things Dr. Kip McKean first discipled me on when I was serving in his ministry in Los Angeles, California was my need to have more "life force." He pointed out that when Jesus was in a room, you knew He was there. Life force comes by walking powerfully with God and consciously focusing on being zealous. I am a product of discipling in this area of my life; anything forceful that is seen now in my life has come from years of discipling and pushing myself into uncomfortable situations. Let me say it very clearly here: There is no cool way to share your faith, and you probably will never get to a place where it is natural or easy. I think this is because God wants us to have to rely on Him. With that said, I do believe God led me to a tool that can help you overcome that initial fear.

The Bible says, *"Appoint three men from each tribe. I will send them out to make a survey of the land and to write a description of it, according to the inheritance of each. Then they will return to me."* **(Joshua 18:4)** I can remember reading this one day and thinking, "We need to survey our campuses!" Clearly, my conclusion was not based on this verse's best exegesis (ok, so it is not at all). Yet, it at least put the idea in my head. I had seen other religious groups do surveys to generate conversation about one's eternity and thought, "Couldn't it work for disciples?" Anyone on a college campus knows that many people are constantly handing out flyers for events, requesting signatures on petitions for political change, and proselytizing recruits for fraternities, sororities, and clubs. It is in this culture that the campus leader can take advantage of the survey.

I came up with three questions for a survey that help generate great conversation. 1. What do you believe about the afterlife? (Reincarnation, heaven/hell, just rot in the ground, etc.) 2. Does that belief affect how you live day to day? Is it something you are aware of when making choices? 3. On what do you base that belief? (Bible, Quran, holy writing, science, tradition, family, etc.) The last question gets them to think about the origins of their religious beliefs. You can come up with your own questions if you desire. Regardless, it creates an opportunity to discuss your faith with them and invite them to a Bible Talk. You just need a notepad and a pen and to stand in a high-traffic area on campus and stop people by saying, "I'm with a [name of group] on campus, and we are just taking a quick three-question survey on what students believe on campus. Question one is…" Notice you do not ask them if they want to take the survey; you boldly go right into it. You lead the situation when it comes to cold-contact evangelism. The survey helps if they end up studying the Bible because you will know what they believe from the questions. The point is not so much the questions and answers but to get a good conversation going. It is an icebreaker of sorts to get straight to the point.

The Three Question Campus Survey

1. Do you believe in an afterlife? (Heaven, hell, reincarnation, nothing after, etc.)

2. Does this belief affect how you live morally? Is it something you are aware of when making choices?

3. On what do you base that belief? (Religious text, tradition, personal experience, family, etc.)

You must follow the Spirit and bring the conversation to a place of decision. The challenge is to get them to commit to coming to a Bible study or event by getting their phone number. The surveys are incredibly helpful for new disciples. I still use them to this day, as by nature, I can struggle with being timid. I am not as naturally social as my wife is (God knew what I needed), so for me, it helps break the ice. I also like it because it gets straight to the point of why you are out there in the first place. Take advantage of this tool and teach it to your campus ministry.

Finally, there is no substitute for the Holy Spirit. The greatest evangelist in the Bible is the Holy Spirit. He is the one who led the early church in their evangelism. The Spirit gave Philip the direction to go near the chariot of the Ethiopian eunuch. (**Acts 8:29**) Therefore, we must be deep in prayer. God will lead us to the people who want to find Him when we are in step with His Spirit.

> *"When you are brought before synagogues, rulers and authorities, do not worry about how you will defend yourselves or what you will say, for the Holy Spirit will teach you at that time what you should say."*
>
> **-LUKE 12:11-12**

These verses give us great comfort on campus when sharing our faith. The Holy Spirit will provide us with words to say. Jesus says not to worry about how we will defend ourselves. In **John 16**, the Holy Spirit has been called in some translations the "Great Comforter." The Holy Spirit cannot comfort someone already comfortable. If we want to see Him work powerfully, we must put ourselves in daring situations that demand His presence as the Apostles had to before the ruling elite. Are you willing to live with the boldness on campus that requires the Holy Spirit to show up?

The verse above also clarifies that they were not to worry about how they would defend themselves when brought before rulers. Specifically, they were not to worry about what they would say. It is in those moments that God loves to come through and work. When we are at our weakest and cannot do it on our own, we need to throw ourselves into daringly bold situations on campus. Demand the presence of the Holy Spirit by living boldly for Christ.

Hopefully, these practical evangelism tools will be as valuable in bearing fruit in your campus ministry as they are in mine. I believe there is much more that could be said about overcoming the blocks that non-Christians throw your way when sharing your faith. We need to continue to share with each other what works as we evangelize all the campuses in our cities. To summarize, remember they must know a *"prophet has been among them,"* which is done by attempting by faith to overcome two or three blocks that are thrown your way. Responding to a question is always the most effective way. If you do not know what to say in response, just remember to ask another question. Ultimately it is love that will convert someone to Christianity. Show a genuine and sincere interest in the person's life that you are sharing with. Finally, surveys are amazing tools to help timid disciples and veteran disciples break the ice in evangelism.

Overcoming "Blocks" With Questions

BLOCK	RESPONSE QUESTION
"I'm not interested."	"What makes you not interested?" "What do you wish the church would change to be more interesting?"
"I'm atheist."	"Have you always been an atheist? When did you become one?" "Have you ever looked into apologetics (evidence for God's existence)? "You have a lot of faith to believe there is no God; what do you base your faith on?"
"I'm not into organized religion."	"What type of religion are you into?" "Are you into disorganized religion?" "How do you define religion?"
"I already attend a church."	"What church do you attend?" "Do you have a discipleship partner?" "Great! Would you be open to meeting up and sharing our faith?"
"You guys have already talked to me."	"How come you have not visited yet?" "Are you open to the idea that God may be trying to get your attention?"
"I'm all set…"	"All set for what specifically?"
"I'm Muslim (or another religion)."	"Are you practicing?" "What do you think our faiths have in common?" "What made you choose that faith?"

10 Questions To Use In "Cold Contact" Evangelism

Here are 10 conversation-starters. You can start by saying, "Excuse me, I wanted to ask…"

1. Are you a spiritual person?
2. What is your purpose in life?
3. What are your thoughts on religion and how it contributes to society?
4. Do you think Christianity is still relevant in our current world?
5. What do you think happens after you die?
6. Who is Jesus Christ to you?
7. Do you currently go to church?
8. How is your relationship with God?
9. What can I pray for you about?
10. What do you think would fix the world's problems?

NOTE: These are just questions, some I use to start a conversation to pique someone's interest in either coming to church, Bible Talk, Bible Study, or getting their phone number. Most want to talk about these types of things!

CHAPTER 8

THEY PUBLICLY MALIGNED THE WAY— PERSECUTION ON CAMPUS

SITTING ACROSS from my college dean and being drilled with questions about what I believe had to be one of the more intimidating moments during my time in college. A few people had become disciples at a small Mainline Church of Christ college I was attending, and it seemed as if it rocked the whole school. The Bible Talk that I was hosting in my dorm room was packed with visitors every week, which was seen as a dangerous threat to the college. I was told I was no longer allowed to host Bible studies on the campus... yes, at a Bible college! Not everyone agreed with the decision, but it became known that Mike Patterson was now part of a "cult." The Bible teaches this is normal and that persecution is promised to those who live a godly life. (**2 Timothy 3:12**) Perhaps Paul recognized this promise would hold true even more for today's college students, who are constantly surrounded by the world and often still dependent on their parents.

PERSECUTION IS PROMISED

Jesus told His disciples that persecution would happen so that they would not fall away. (**John 16:1**) Campus leaders must have the conviction to be like Jesus and do the same. In our First Principles series, an excellent Bible study called "Persecution" is listed as a follow-up study for new Christians. I believe college students must go through this study very early in the study series to prepare them for the Satanic onslaught of persecution. I lead this study after the "Discipleship" study in the series. I may not entirely go into all the doctrinal aspects in the study, depending on the background of the person with whom I am studying, but it is essential to do this study early on. Students, more than ever, will "Google," "Bing," or "ask Siri" to find out information about the church. Since the International Christian Church is striving to be like Jesus, we will be persecuted, and there will continue to be scores of negative articles online about the church. Many, including myself, have made the mistake of not doing the study on persecution early on. Very quickly while studying the Bible or even after someone is baptized, they were taken out of the faith by Satan.

Dear friends, do not be surprised at the fiery ordeal that has come on you to test you, as though something strange were happening to you. But rejoice inasmuch as you participate in the sufferings of Christ, so that you may be overjoyed when His glory is revealed. If you are insulted because of the name of Christ, you are blessed, for the Spirit of glory and of God rests on you. If you suffer, it should not be as a murderer or thief or any other kind of criminal, or even as a meddler.

However, if you suffer as a Christian, do not be ashamed,
but praise God that you bear that name.

-1 PETER 4:12-16

The campus leader who equips the saints with consistent teaching on persecution will have a ministry that is not surprised by persecution.

MANAGE YOUR REPUTATION

At the same time, we must be sure we are doing all we can to avoid unwarranted negativity and unfounded slander about God's Kingdom, His leaders, and the mission of disciples to evangelize our lost world. The Bible is clear that we should not be persecuted for ungodly reasons. **1 Peter 3:15** says, *"But in your hearts revere Christ as Lord. Always be prepared to give an answer to everyone who asks you to give the reason for the hope that you have. But do this with gentleness and respect."* John Causey, who leads our sister church in Chicago, visited Boston a few years ago and challenged our staff to "manage our reputation." Many young college disciples need training on tact in their evangelism not to bring unwarranted "persecution." There must be teaching on how a new convert should present their decision to become a disciple to their parents. Before you baptize a student desiring to become a Christian, make sure they have told their family of their decision. It is better to hit bumps with their family before baptism because if they still put Jesus and His kingdom first amid persecution, you can be sure they have been made into a solid disciple and are fire-tested and ready for baptism. There is nothing more discouraging than baptizing someone who quickly falls away at the persecution of their family. In my years of doing campus ministry, I have found it helpful to build a relationship with the campus students' parents who are not Christians. Let them know you are available to talk if they have any questions or concerns. Reassure them that you want their children to be successful in their academic pursuits. This reassurance eases the parents' anxiety to know there is open communication, and it counteracts the stigma around the cult accusation that we separate students from their families. You will never be able to avoid persecution, as it is a promise from God to true disciples, but tactfulness can go a long way in allowing the faith of your students to grow stronger in the early stages of their walk with God.

INTEGRITY

It is essential to understand your rights at the college where you are ministering. Private colleges will be a little stricter than public universities. Jesus said, *"I am sending you out like sheep among wolves. Therefore be as shrewd as snakes and as innocent as doves."* (**Matthew 10:16**) Jesus acknowledges that the ministry is dangerous. Wolves are out to devour us, and this requires us to be shrewd (cunning, wise, smart) and at the same time innocent. We must present ourselves in a way to outsiders that will not be foolish. Then they can have nothing wrong to say about us, even if they disagree with our convictions from the Bible.

Another form of unwarranted persecution is when we do not disciple our students to do well in their college studies. Many zealous students are genuinely so fired up (and rightfully so) about their newfound relationship with God and His church that some can even literally want to drop out of school because they see it as a worthless pursuit. They see pursuing the ministry as a more worthwhile use of their time. As spiritual as that may sound to some, dropping out of college is not spiritual. My strong conviction is that God put them at that college to reach the students there. How can students reach out to their classmates if they are failing their classes? How can they reach their parents if they want to quit? When it comes to raising up leaders, the whole premise of campus ministry is that the discipline it takes to be in college alone is training for the discipline it takes to be in the full-time ministry. Their classes are also where they get all their connections and relationships to be able to make disciples. In our teaching, we need to stress that school is part of their discipleship. If someone becomes a Christian and their grades drop, something is wrong in their relationship with God. The apostle Paul encourages us to do everything *"as working for the Lord."* (**Colossians 3:23**) Everything includes keeping a high standard of excellence in the students' academic pursuits. The campus leader must care about this aspect of their ministry, which will help curtail persecution.

Once someone becomes a Christian, they now represent Christ in every area of their life. **Colossians 3:23** says, *"Whatever you do, work at it with all your heart, as working for the Lord, not for human masters."* I will not allow students to be Bible Talk leaders who do not excel in their schoolwork. When final exams come around, you may decide to have a study devotional for your Friday Devotional, or perhaps your evangelist allows your midweek that week to be a "study midweek." Study nights convey to students that the church is concerned about how well they do in their studies. Remember, we are building God's Kingdom. If they do well in their studies and graduate, many become doctors, lawyers, and professionals who can help build God's Church financially and make it more attractive to the world. Campus leaders who unintentionally encourage students to put their school studies on the back burner in the name of "seeking first the kingdom" do not value the excellence God expects of us in all areas. Students need to see their schoolwork as part of their Christianity and even their testimony to the lost.

Some students have fallen away because they feel overwhelmed by schoolwork, believing the church was taking too much of their time. I remember having an evangelism campaign at the University of Florida that required a lot of time, and one of the new sisters was struggling. She did not feel like her schoolwork was valued and sadly fell away. Students must see their academia as part of their discipleship. Fundamentally, they do not see their entire identity in Christ when their grades are failing, that they are a disciple of Jesus in everything. They tend to compartmentalize their lives amongst discipleship, schoolwork, and other activities as if being a disciple is just another "piece of the pie" of their life. When students develop a conviction that the *"Christ, who is your life"* (**Colossians 3:4**) is the same Christ who did *"everything well,"* (**Mark 7:37**) they will see the need to excel in all areas of their own lives. They are in Christ as a student, they are in Christ as an athlete, they are in Christ as an employee, and they are in Christ in the ministry. Discipleship consumes the entire life, not just when they are at church.

One student who exemplifies this attitude of excellence is Christina Wilson, who currently serves as a campus minister alongside her husband, Jordan Wilson. Christina became a Christian during my time as a campus minister at the University of Florida in Gainesville. Upon graduating, she was accepted into graduate school at Harvard University; ironically, at the same time, Chenelle and I were asked to move to Boston to serve the church there. Under an extremely demanding schedule and intense course work, Christina not only graduated from her Harvard Graduate Program, but she also graduated from ICCM at the same time! Christina has always been one of the most fruitful sisters I have ever met. She always put God first and sought much advice about her schedule while excelling in her academics. Christina graduated with a degree in architecture, beginning work at an incredibly lucrative job. When called to go into full-time ministry, she willingly gave up her secular career to advance God's Kingdom. Students with life examples like Christina's inspire us and make it very clear that there is no excuse for not being excellent in academics as a disciple of Jesus.

When one understands their identity, it is no longer a choice between church or their homework. The church must come first because of their identity in Christ, and their homework will be excelled at the same time because Christ expects them to excel in all things as working for Him. Use your devotional time to teach students how to be disciplined in their schedules. Do not accept the excuse that the church keeps them too busy to do their homework. I have done a whole devotional where I write on a chalkboard an example planner and teach the students how to prioritize and schedule their life. Do not assume everyone knows how to do this.

Persecution is promised to anyone who lives a godly life. The early Christians never sought after persecution, but at the same time, they did not pray for it to go away. Instead, they prayed for boldness to endure the onslaught of persecution from Satan. (**Acts 4:23-31**) The campus leader must disciple his ministry to be tactful and represent God's Kingdom in a way that no one can accuse of being wrong (though they will regardless). We can do this by teaching our students to excel in their schoolwork and building strong relationships with their families. Most importantly, we teach about persecution constantly, which equips the disciples to endure through it. God's people always thrived under persecution, and they will thrive again in this century as we sweep college campuses with the gospel around the world.

Christina Wilson, a daughter in the faith to the Pattersons, was converted at the University of Florida, graduated from Harvard with a Master's in Architecture, and is pictured here with the author after receiving her bachelor's degree in ministry from the International College of Christian Ministry (ICCM). She now serves in the full-time ministry in the Boston church.

CHAPTER 9

HE TOOK THE DISCIPLES WITH HIM AND HAD DISCUSSIONS DAILY— CAMPUS PRESENCE

PAUL TOOK THE DISCIPLES with him to the Lecture Hall of Tyrannus. Most likely, these were the same twelve who had been converted in **Acts 19:1-6** when he started the church in Ephesus. Some may have been numbered among the Ephesian church elders whom Paul addresses in **Acts 20** three years later. Reflecting on his three years leading the church in Ephesus, Paul writes about his discipling of these men: *"So be on your guard! Remember that for three years I never stopped warning each of you night and day with tears."* **(Acts 20:31)** To build a powerful campus ministry that would evangelize all of first-century Asia, Paul understood the need for daily discipleship. This three-year stay involved individual discipleship (*"each of you"*) and group discipleship, as they were together daily having *"daily discussions."* Discipleship is not just a once-a-week meeting or a Bible study. Although those are essential, it is taking the disciples with you as you do ministry to watch and imitate. Your campus ministry will never see the forceful advancement you desire if you do not have daily Bible Talks and discipling. When we are talking about discipling, we are talking about influencing personal spiritual growth and the training of student leadership. Paul's effective church-building strategies were a huge part of his heroic leadership. Let's look at the following key components of college ministry that will surely maximize your disciples' presence on campus.

BECOMING A HERO

After David slew Goliath, he became a hero to God's people. Eventually, Saul put him in charge of leading the troops in a conspiracy to get David killed, but he still had victories despite the odds and despite being new. Many campus leaders can learn from David's refusal to make excuses for why he could not lead. The Bible says, *"But all Israel and Judah loved David, because he led them in their campaigns."* (**1 Samuel 18:16**) David was a hero because he led on the front lines and provided victory for God's people. The city of Jerusalem was eventually called the City of David! Indeed, God stoops down to make His humble servants great.

I believe the most significant spiritual leaders are legendary and have an almost mythical status in God's Kingdom. This fame is not because of pride or because they sought it, but because of their leadership and extraordinary exploits for God. You must become a hero to your campus ministry. You must be a miracle worker and do acts that no one has ever done before. For David, it started with a sling and five smooth stones when he ran into an enemy territory full of faith to slay Goliath. No one in Israel, including King Saul, a giant of a man himself, was willing to do this.

What heroic act do you need to do in your ministry to inspire those you lead? Maybe you need to do some street preaching? Yes, it may not be effective, but will it not inspire those you lead? Maybe you need to have a crazy campaign that sounds impossible, but through your strategic leadership and the principles learned in this paper, you accomplish it! It could be sharing your faith with 100 people a day. I mean, who else is doing that? Maybe you need to convert an opinion leader. David believed that with God, nothing was impossible. Heroic leadership is vital as it inspires a culture of imitation. Everyone should want to be like the campus leader. Discipleship is not complicated. It is simply calling people to follow you as you follow Christ. (**1 Corinthians 11:1**)

The author with a few of his heroes in the faith (Dr. Andrew Smellie, Dr. Raul Moreno, and Dr. Tim Kernan) while doing campus ministry at Cal-State.

AUTHORITY TO LEAD

Now that you have become a hero to your campus ministry, you have the moral authority to call people to action. Authority is a touchy subject for many people. Authority must be established in your ministry so there can be unity. Without the campus leader's authority established, students will not be obedient to your evangelism campaigns, dating guidelines, Bible Talk setups, etc. The leader's personal example is the most inspirational way to establish their authority. Secondly, I have found that if you teach on authority, people will obey. Teaching on submission may sound simplistic, but the fact is, in America, a nation founded on rebellion, submission and humility do not come naturally. Many students do not know the authority that spiritual leaders have in their life, and if you do not teach them, they never will. I do many lessons on how God chooses leadership and that grumbling against God's leaders is grumbling against God. (**Exodus 16**) The Bible is clear that disciples are to be obedient to church leadership in every area unless, of course, they were to call them to disobey the Bible, which would be a sin. (**Hebrews 13:17**)

The campus leader may desire to take a group of college students and move them to a different part of campus, have them move into a dorm to evangelize that dorm, or suggest some sort of other life change to propel God's Kingdom. But if the students do not understand your authority, they will have difficulty obeying such life-changing situations. If anyone in effect has to say, "Obey me because I'm the leader and the Bible says so," they have lost the battle and are setting up their ministry for rebellion. Although that statement is true, Jesus led from a place of servitude. It is easy to obey your hero, and that is why you must be heroic in your leadership if you are to have authority. The disciples trusted Jesus had their best interests in mind because of how much He loved them, so when He used His authority to call them to action, they were obedient. If you have taught about authority and called people to obedience and still feel there is disobedience in your ministry, you may need to look long and hard on serving and loving your people. God establishes authority in His kingdom, and we must not be ashamed to call people to the obedience that comes from faith.

When I ran track, it was easier to listen to the coaches who also were active runners. They kept themselves in shape, could do the same running drills, and showed us by example the correct form to have over the hurdles by actually doing it. I could follow them and respect what they said because they had the example to back it up. The coaches who might be out of shape and maybe ran track when they were young were harder to follow since the example was lacking. I still needed to obey them because of the authority they had if I was to be on the team but having that life example sure made it easier. The campus minister must lead from the front with a strong example in his evangelism, prayer life, and devotional life.

Interestingly, the Bible calls us to *"obedience that comes from faith."* **(Romans 1:5)** Faith is tied to obedience. The more we have a great, faithful vision for our campus ministry, the more the students will obey the vision. For example, as Paul said to King Agrippa, *"I was not disobedient to the vision."* **(Acts 26:19)** At the University of Florida, I put before the ministry the "Campus Conquest" vision. It was a vision to have a Campus Bible Talk at every population center on campus. A map was handed out with our targeted locations and the plan to make the vision a reality. The students then felt compelled to submit to the authority of the campaigns and plans we had since they all contributed to our single-focused vision. Faithful vision brings unity and submission.

Paul exhibited this authority by taking his disciples with him to the Lecture Hall of Tyrannus and having daily Bible Talks. Notice it did not say, "Paul asked his disciples if they would come with him," it just says they went. This is the result of Paul having a great example and great vision that demanded obedience.

FIND YOUR "SOLOMON'S COLONNADE"

In more than one chapter of Acts we find the disciples meeting in one location to discuss issues of faith daily. These "fellowship hubs" were evidently an important part of how the early church started! An incredible conversion tool of the early church was having hot spots or places you could always find disciples meeting amongst population centers. **Acts 5:12** says, *"The apostles performed many signs and wonders among the people. And all the believers used to meet together in Solomon's Colonnade."* Solomon's Colonnade was a place in the temple courts where you could always find the disciples. After a long day of work in Jerusalem as a Christian, you could come here to find encouragement and discussions with non-Christians. Non-Christian Jews would see the love of the disciples who came to the temple to worship and eventually become disciples themselves because this love impacted them.

The fellowship hub is a key to building a campus ministry presence. You must find a population center where students hang out. Usually, this is a dining area or student union that most students walk through or hang out in. I would advise having daily Bible Talks in the same place publicly during high-traffic hours. You want to do your Bible studies in this area and have discipling times in this location. The disciples will then begin to hang out in this spot often. Their friends from class will see them and stop to say "hi," giving you a chance to meet them as well. You should be known as the campus minister, even among the non-Christians on campus.

It should be noted that disciples on college campuses where they have been banned or undergone intense persecution may need to use caution on this point and not do Bible studies with non-Christians publicly. Other "campus ministers" from false doctrine religious groups have been known to pull those they see studying with the campus leader aside and afterward try to poison them towards our ministries. Regardless, it is still essential to create a refuge and hang-out spot for disciples to come to, and it creates organic growth while producing new studies for your ministry.

STUDY WITH EVERYONE

The campus leader must be involved in most of the studies with non-Christians. Too many campus leaders make the mistake of thinking they are to function as the church evangelist; they select only a few guys they disciple and overly structure their ministries initially, which is a fatal mistake. You need to be the one who is involved in as many of the studies with non-Christians as possible. Campus leaders who are young, single, without kids, and working full-time for the church can disciple 12 people. Being a hero and creating a Solomon's Colonnade requires being on campus all day and leading from the front. Please do not become the armchair leader or manager who directs his disciples on what to do through his phone. Paul took the disciples with him so they could see his life in action as he preached the Word, and this is biblical discipleship. The 12 he took with him, as said earlier, naturally became the leaders he needed to lead the Ephesus church. Do not worry about who your "12" or chosen leaders will be. It will be obvious! As the ministry grows, you will have to get advice on organizing things structurally to be united with your lead evangelist. Still, one campus leader can handle 30 disciples and personally touch each one (not disciple everyone). Discipleship groups are also necessary on campus. Having a men's campus discipleship group during Women's Midweek can be productive and vice-versa for the women.

THE CAMPUS LEADER IS A COACH

As the campus leader, you want to take on the mindset of being a coach to your ministry, specifically those you are discipling. When leading a Bible study with a non-Christian, you lead it first and let the disciple in the study know you will have them lead it next time. When that time comes, you watch them lead it, then afterward pull them aside and tell them what they did positively in the study and how they could grow next time they lead the study. After every welcome, communion, or any kind of speech, pull them aside and coach them. Every meeting is an opportunity for discipling. Use the fellowship to coach your students to make sure they are out of themselves and fellowshipping non-Christians. Tell one of those you are discipling to have a deep conversation with a weaker disciple in the fellowship. You can use the fellowship as an incredible time to train your disciples. Challenge them to sit by disciples they do not know. Encourage them to ask the weak, struggling sister on an encouragement date, or if they are a sister, the weak, struggling brother. We often do not use this incredible time God has given us to train our disciples in the Lord.

DAILY BIBLE TALKS

The disciples had discussions daily. In modern terms, they had daily Bible Talks. There are two types of Bible Talks: 1) The Normal Bible Talk—which has the purpose of growth and building a family to keep new converts faithful. 2) The Campus Express Bible Talk—this is a Bible Talk that is 10 to 15 minutes long, usually in the afternoon, in a high-traffic population center on campus, aimed at setting up Bible studies. This Bible Talk should not be an "official church Bible Talk" that members are placed in, as it has no value in building a family. The Campus Express Bible Talk is a daily Bible Talk that the campus leader or other interns should lead, and they should grab as many disciples as possible to join. The disciples meet around an hour or 30 minutes before starting the Bible Talk and blitz the population center, inviting as many as possible to come. The leader then does a short and powerful discussion geared at getting visitors to study the Bible, and members break up afterward to do "Seeking God" studies with those who came out. In my experience, these Bible Talks usually do not get the "Opinion Leaders" (those of influence on campus) yet are extraordinary at increasing your ministry. By having a bigger ministry, you now have something to bring opinion leaders to, and they will see the kingdom through the love the disciples have for each other. **(John 13:34-35)**

THE CHARIOT RIDE

Another great tool in campus ministry is the "Chariot Ride." **Acts 8:26-39** chronicles the conversion of the Ethiopian Eunuch, who was open to the Scriptures and converted after a chariot ride with Philip. The Chariot Ride is when you gather all the non-Christians who have been studying the Bible and know they need to become disciples but who are dragging their feet slightly. Then bring them into someone's home and have the leaders prepare an awesome meal for everyone in attendance. Those who have been involved in the studies come with the non-Christian. After a fantastic meal, the campus leader gives a sermon on hell, discipleship, the cross, and total commitment

Neal Patel was converted at a "Chariot Ride" in three days at the University of Florida, completed his Masters at Boston University, and then moved with the Pattersons to New York City to help them do campus work at Columbia University.

to God and His church. It is a lesson done with passion, laying out the whole gospel message. Following the sermon, two campus disciples are chosen to share their testimony. I recommend having one "pagan" testimony and one "religious" testimony. Be strategic about whom you choose so they can relate to those that are present. Once the Chariot Ride event is over, the non-Christians should be called to a decision and a plan should be made for when they are getting baptized. In some cases, they might choose to be baptized that night if they are willing to give up everything and finish the studies (or at least the studies' main doctrinal points)!

DORMITORY (DORM) BIBLE TALKS

Having daily discussions certainly creates a presence on campus, but what else might impact the campus? Dorm Bible Talks get you into the very fabric of the college. These can be highly effective, especially if you have campus students who live in the dorms. It is wise to consider asking enrolled students to sacrifice an apartment's comforts and purposely move into the dorms to create a campus presence. Dorm Bible Talks were highly effective decades ago and still can be effective. The challenge we have today is security is a lot tighter than it once was on campus. If your campus ministry is used to only doing "Campus Express" type Bible Talks, Dorm Bible Talks are an opportunity for your campus workers to expand their ministry skills and learn new "fishing techniques." Visitors will come from the relationships that students are building in their dorm, classes, activities, etc., and most likely will not be the last-minute person you just grab. The Bible Talk leader must daily work the Bible Talk to have commitments who are planning on coming. Knocking every door in a dormitory can also be highly effective. The campus leader can develop an evangelism plan to get to every dorm on his campus, similar to our movement's Crown of Thorns plan to inspire the Christians. This type of vision can be extremely exciting and create momentum in the ministry.

Another opportunity to build longevity in the ministry is sharing your faith with freshmen. There are usually freshmen dorms that can be great fishing holes to reach out to students. The first couple weeks of the new college semester are essential to getting these students, as they are looking for friends and social groups to join. If you are a club on campus, it is essential to look into doing a "Club Day" or "Tabling Day" that most colleges have for the freshmen to explore different campus clubs and sign up. Find out when the move-in day for the dorms is and offer a ministry to help students move into their dorm rooms. This is another fantastic opportunity to meet new students and get their contact information to come out to a Bible Talk or study. Plan many visitor-friendly events those first two weeks of the campus semester, such as barbeques, ultimate frisbee, volleyball, game nights, etc.

CAMPUS COLONNADE

When Paul was in Athens, the intellectual capital of his day, he found that people enjoyed *"talking about and listening to the latest ideas"* (**Acts 17:21**) just as they do on the campuses of our day. I am in debt to Nick Enfantino, who introduced me to the concept of the "Campus Colonnade" while he was the campus minister at Columbia University. Though Columbia University is an Ivy League college that traditionally is more difficult to baptize at, Nick, in one semester, baptized six students at Columbia! No wonder he went on

Nick Enfantino's "Campus Colonnade" poster at Columbia
University. He baptized five students in five months
at CU and now leads the Philadelphia ICC!

to plant the Philadelphia church and is slated to lead the Bahrain
International Christian Church!

The "Campus Colonnade" was held once a semester on campus. Being
a student organization helped as they would fund an incredible feast.
A controversial topic about Christianity would be taught to pique
students' interest to sign up to attend. Nick had me speak when the
topic was on how Christianity is relevant to college students' lives.
Once I started leading the campus ministry at Columbia University,
we did one on the theme "God is Dead," taken from the German

philosopher Friedrich Nietzsche. Flyers were put all around campus with big words that said "God is Dead" with other controversial cultural issues and was the perfect event for an Ivy League campus and always a lot of fun. We must constantly come up with new ways and opportunities to reach more students for Christ.

The author speaks at a "Campus Colonnade" on the theme "God is Dead." The focus centered on both this philosophical misconception and the intellectual reasons why God is NOT dead, ultimately concluding that it logically makes sense to follow him.

INTRAMURAL SPORTS

Intramural sports are also a great networking opportunity for evangelism. Colleges allow students to form sports teams and compete in competitions with other teams. The student disciples can create a sports team and get non-Christians to join or use it to reach out to those they face in competition. The campus leader should do what they can to stay in shape and participate in athletic events for the ministry. I am not much of a team sports player, though I was an athlete in college and high school as a part of the track team. Over time, I had to learn to put away my insecurity and play sports with the disciples. I even ended up enjoying it a ton. When we have a basketball event or ultimate frisbee game, it inspires the students to see their church or campus leader playing.

WOMEN'S MINISTRY

The women's ministry is also crucial to building a powerful presence on campus. Many campus ministries miss out on the opportunity of having All Women Bible Talks allowing the sisters in Christ to raise up and learn leadership. Many women on our campuses desire leadership and have been impacted by feminist-type ideas. They have been repelled by the religious groups that suppress women or misinterpret what the Bible teaches about women's roles. God's Kingdom offers an incredible place for powerful women who are opinion leaders to use their gifts to lead other women to God. Campus leaders who lift up the women's ministry by constantly creating opportunities for them to lead will see God multiply their ministry much more than those who do not. One example of this type of leadership opportunity is the creation of All-Women's Bible Talks.

In this chapter, we have talked about how to disciple students and create a powerful campus presence. Campus leaders must imitate our brother Paul by taking the disciples with them and creating daily discussions. This integration of the students into the very fabric of college life will forcefully advance your campus ministry. Leading *Project Tyrannus* takes authority, training, and great faith. In many ways, it takes even more faith to maintain this presence, which we will now address in the next chapter.

CHAPTER 10

THIS WENT ON FOR TWO YEARS—CONSISTENCY

SOMEONE ONCE SAID, "The most radical thing you can do is to be consistent." Luke tells us in Acts 19 that Paul had daily discussions on the campus in Ephesus for two years. Paul's consistency was radical, maintaining the same thing every day and not growing weary for two whole years. Later, Paul calls the Galatians to his example by writing, *"Let us not become weary in doing good, for at the proper time we will reap a harvest if we do not give up."* **(Galatians 6:9)** This type of consistency takes a radical discipline in one's lifestyle. The question is not whether you believe in the principles described in this book, but rather are you willing to pay the price of putting them into practice? Paul paid the price of consistency every day for two years! What could God do if you were consistent in your schedule, spending time on campus every day? What are some of the other things we should do consistently every day as campus leaders?

It should go without saying that the basics of being a Christian, such as reading your Bible, prayer, confession, etc., should be done every day. Jesus was clear that one could not be a disciple unless they carry their cross daily. **(Luke 9:23)** What should the campus leaders do every day beyond the usual daily habits of a disciple of Christ? The following list is not exhaustive but, based on my experience, includes the essential ingredients for a daily recipe for campus ministry success.

CONSISTENT PRAYER LIFE

...and will give our attention to prayer and the ministry of the Word.

-ACTS 6:4

When the church in Jerusalem was growing rapidly, the Apostles had to choose men to do specific tasks to stay focused on "... *prayer and the ministry of the Word.*" It is crucial to notice that the Bible says they devoted themselves first to prayer and then the ministry. Many ambitious campus workers burn out spiritually because they devote themselves first to the ministry, giving what is left over of themselves to prayer. Reordering this Scripture is always a recipe for spiritual burnout. God is moved by the prayer life of the campus minister, and He alone can move the ministry. We can assume that Paul did not evangelize all of Asia from the lecture hall by only doing ministry daily, but that he had a radically consistent prayer life. **(Romans 1:8-10; 2 Corinthians 13:7; Ephesians 1:15-23; Ephesians 3:14-21; Philippians 1:3-6, 9-11; 1 Thessalonians 1:2-3; Philemon 1:4-6)** Paul had influence by praying and moving the heart of our Father to work on his behalf. How is your prayer life?

Are you praying grand, global, earth-shaking prayers for revival on your campus or just squeezing in a quick religious prayer for a few minutes before you go to bed? This book has taught many methods, strategies, and keys to effective ministry, but I put before you, it will all be in vain without devotion to prayer. (**Colossians 4:2**)

Ronald Clay (right), a Berklee College of Music student, shares with joy as he gets ready to baptize Joshua Hoggard (left), who also attends the same college. Both of them have gone on to become great leaders in the campus ministry.

CONSISTENT BIBLE READING

Consistently reading the Bible is just as important as prayer. Today there are so many distractions from the Word of God. Another temptation of an ambitious ministry worker is first checking the phone in the morning instead of talking to God. The flesh wants to respond to emails and social media notifications, as well as begin planning our day before we spend time in God's presence. I want to challenge you to have the conviction to not communicate with anyone until you have first communicated with God. Create this discipline in your life daily. Prayer is talking to God, and reading is listening to God. In every great relationship, communication flows both ways and happens daily. In his NT epistles, Paul quotes from the Old Testament 131 times, showing us that the Word of God was hidden in his heart. **(Psalm 119:11)**

CONSISTENT FOLLOW-UP

Next, the campus worker should do a daily follow-up with those he has reached out to by setting aside an hour of his time to text message and call those whose numbers he received from his sharing times. During the follow-up, you should pray for your new friends—then you can continue to set up Bible studies or get commitments to the meetings of the body. I find having an organized system, as mentioned earlier, is vital to this. I must see the list of names of the people I'm working with every day. You should share your faith with multitudes of students daily. Of course, the disciple shares his faith every day, but the leader shares his faith with many people every day. The campus leader or worker should be sharing with hundreds and hundreds of people every week as a daily habit and part of one's lifestyle. Do we say we want to build campus ministries of thousands but then resist sharing with thousands? Reaching thousands will take keeping your schedule full of appointments with non-Christians. The full-time campus worker should have a minimum of eight appointments in the day. Additionally, every day there needs to be contact with the men or women you disciple and lead, encouraging them, feeding them spiritually, and putting them to work on campus. With these spiritual disciplines of leadership built into your life consistently, like Paul, you will see incredible results and begin to impact the world!

Without prayer, the tools learned in this book will prove useless. Prayer moves God; only God moves the ministry.

CHAPTER 11

HEARD THE WORD OF THE LORD— GLOBAL EVANGELISM

ASIA MINOR, which corresponds to modern-day Turkey, was completely evangelized because Paul decided to take his ministry to a learning center—the Lecture Hall of Tyrannus in Ephesus. Likely, Paul knew he could find those with hearts not only open to the gospel but also to his vision to evangelize the entire world. What started in Ephesus, the capital of Asia Minor, would be the key to so many other church plantings. Paul preached the Word of the Lord to his "campus ministry" and it always centered on world evangelism in his generation. **(Acts 9:15)**

The author, with the Gainesville mission team getting ready to be sent
out to the University of Florida. This church planted the seeds
for church plantings in Miami and Tampa.

World evangelism in this generation is the motivating vision of
God's people and must be for our campus ministries. Many do not
understand the urgency of the timeframe given by Jesus of "this
generation." **Matthew 28:18-20** teaches that Jesus wanted His disciples to get to all nations in their lifetime. Earlier, He had told His
disciples that the gospel would be preached to all nations and the
end would come. (**Matthew 24:14**) The end in context was referring
to the destruction of Jerusalem in 70AD. Jesus told the disciples
when the church began in 29AD that His movement would start in
Jerusalem, expand to Samaria, and reach the ends of the earth. (**Acts
1:8**) The only generation that you can obey Jesus in is your generation. In the twenty-first century, we only have our generation in
which to obey Jesus and get to all nations. The first-century disciples quickly spread throughout all the world, and Paul would write

in **Colossians 1:23** in 60-62 AD that every creature under heaven had heard about the church! Shortly after, in 70 AD, Jerusalem is destroyed, fulfilling Jesus' prophecy. Biblically, it is clear the first-century church evangelized the nations in their generation, and we need to in our generation!

Many campus ministers preach that disciples are to share their faith and evangelize their college campus. Still, they fail to preach the vision of evangelizing all nations in their lifetime. If you do not teach that all disciples are responsible to evangelize the world in a generation, it produces a lack of urgency to win souls and an unwillingness to sacrifice for the church universal. The whole reason Paul was at the lecture hall was to evangelize the world. Paul and the disciples did not keep all the new converts there in Ephesus nor did they attempt to build a mega-campus ministry or mega-church. Think of how many of those originally converted in Ephesus were sent out, so that in two years, all of Asia was evangelized!

I believe our campus ministry seminars, like the International Campus Leadership Seminar (ICLS), are crucial for creating a sense of fellowship among students from around the world and equipping them to be abundantly fruitful. These seminars help students build relationships that will last a lifetime and maintain the unity of the worldwide movement since many will go on to serve in many leadership roles in our churches. It is imperative to call as many students as possible to attend these life-changing events, which fuel the fire to reach the world in our generation with the gospel of Jesus.

We need to reach our generation because it is the only generation that we are in control of. Moses was an incredible leader who had the foresight to invest in the youth of his time by raising up Joshua. Despite that first-generation dying in the desert, because of Moses' conviction to invest in the youth, Joshua led that second generation into the Promise Land. **(Exodus 33:11; Numbers 27:15-18)** We must invest in raising up leaders in our campus ministry if the future generations are also to have hope. One major failure of Joshua was that he did not raise up leaders. Thus, when Joshua died, the future generations failed to follow God. Campus ministry is so crucial to raising up new leaders for this generation and future generations to come.

When I was leading at the University of Florida, an inspirational campus devotional that we held involved separating the student disciples into groups, each group being given a different major city from various nations. They then had to take the next week and research this city and nation as if their group was going on a mission team to plant a church in that city. At the next devotional, they had to present their strategy to plant this city and evangelize it. It was a powerful way to put world missions into the hearts of the campus disciples and constantly remember why we are doing what we do. There should be preached into existence a culture celebrating the excitement of being sent on a mission team someday. Students from different nations and campus opinion leaders who experience this visionary and international atmosphere will be converted as global disciples, expecting to reach the world for Jesus.

Any major college contains foreign exchange students who need to be taught that they are the hope for their nation to be evangelized. The cost for these young men and women to become disciples is to be willing to go back to their homeland and preach the gospel. I'll never forget taking the disciples street preaching in Boston and a young woman named Fang walking up to listen to the preaching. Intrigued by what was being said, she asked one of the disciples, "How do I become a part of this?" She then came to church and studied the Bible. Fang was baptized into Christ and would eventually start taking classes at Harvard. When the call came for her to move to Sydney, which oversees the work in Asia, she responded

The author and his pregnant wife participated in Moscow, Russia, at the Eurasian Missions Conference. The only way campus ministry will genuinely impact the world is by being part of a global movement.

to the call with a willingness to go back to her homeland to preach the Word. Since then, she has gotten married and was appointed a Women's Ministry Leader! Our campus ministries must reflect the city's diversity and reach those foreign exchange students. Creating diversity takes teaching disciples to share with people who are out of their comfort zone. It also takes time and patience if there is a language barrier.

The investment needed is the same with opinion leaders. Athletes, those in fraternities and sororities, honor students, those in student government, presidents of clubs, etc., are excellent conversions as they can bring so many to Christ. God gifted them with leadership skills meant to be used in His kingdom to bring Him glory. I believe it is the campus leader's responsibility to lead the way in sharing their faith with international students and opinion leaders. It's time to be bold and unashamed and ensure that world evangelism is in the heart of every campus disciple!

CHAPTER 12

REACHING THIS GENERATION

ALTHOUGH THE GOSPEL has not changed, nor has it lost any of its power, certainly times have changed. Every generation places value on different ideas of what is important to them. Today's college student is much different from the college student of the 1960s. Social media has become a primary mode of human connection. Also, atheism is on the rise and promoted at Ivy League colleges and public universities. In my thirteen years doing campus ministry, I have noticed a shift in values. There are both positives and negatives, but as stated at the beginning of this book, the opportunities are enormous for us! I believe that to reach this generation, we will have to make some changes in our approach.

Jesus taught the road is narrow to eternal life. Indeed, the doctrine of Jesus has an exclusive nature to it. The exclusive message is unchanging, and disciples cannot compromise on the truth: The blood of Christ saves only baptized disciples. At the same time, His message has a very inclusive spirit being that all mankind is made in God's image. (**Genesis 1:28**) It is either exclusivity or inclusivity that generations have put a value on. The pendulum has swung back and forth depending on the time. When I was in high school and college, the value was put on being in the "cool crowd" or the "in-group." The cliquish environment was very evident at lunchtime in high school. The athletes, cheerleaders, and popular kids sat together while the gaming "nerds," who were usually made fun of by the popular kids, also assembled.

Exclusivity is now revolting to our current generation. Inclusivity of all is the popular message seen clearly in many of the movements today, such as the gay rights or LGBTQ movement. It is no longer acceptable to talk in such black-and-white terms about much of anything anymore. Whether this is good or bad is not the point of this book. We need to look at how this impacts our campus evangelism with the shifting values. Up until now, I believe we have emphasized the exclusive aspect of Jesus' message in our presentation. While God's love is all-inclusive, a covenantal relationship with Him is exclusive. There are those who will accept its conditions and those who will not. In this way, heaven is exclusive and will never change, but our approach can change how we share the gospel to emphasize its inclusive qualities.

Our society has changed. In an American city, the Folsom Street Fair has people come naked, dressed in "bondage" sex gear, and engaging in public masturbation, all in the middle of the day in our country. There were reports of multiple minors and even one dad who brought his two-year-old dressed in bondage gear. A reporter asked the dad if it is wrong to have his daughter there. He responded,

"Every parent must decide for themselves what is right for them. And I respect that. And we decide that this is right for our children."[16] This story reflects that this current generation is increasingly immersed in a society that does not have a standard of truth.

When you approach a college student today to study the Bible, many times they think these are truths we can each individually decide to have or not. They believe there is no absolute truth, which ironically is an absolute truth statement in and of itself! Jesus spoke in absolutes—heaven and hell exist, you are building on the rock or the sand, you are either in light or darkness. Yet, students with today's "post-truth" mindset have a hard time even beginning to process Jesus' teachings because of how they have been influenced culturally. I want to propose a few minor changes we should prayerfully consider reaching out to a "post-truth" college generation more effectively.

INCLUSIVE FELLOWSHIP

When we share our faith with a student on campus, we have this thinking that they are not a member of the church until baptism. Biblically, this is absolutely true. We even talk about students as "visitors" until they are baptized into Christ. I heard someone say the church can function like a gym. Until you have a membership, you cannot use the equipment. We can feel that until people are baptized, they cannot participate in the activities of the church. Indeed, only baptized disciples can lead in the church in any authoritative

---

16 William Love, "Folsom: A Perfect Place for Kids?" East Bay Times, September 29, 2005, http://www.eastbaytimes.com/2005/09/29/folsom-a-perfect-place-for-kids.

role (speak, lead songs, etc.), but we must ask ourselves if there are opportunities we are missing to include those who are interested in fellowship with us? This mentality stops student disciples from inviting their friends over to their household meetings, MERCY Events, family times, and other activities that pull people into the inner workings of the lifestyle of disciples. The exclusive spirit is a subtle thing, but I believe people are spiritual and can sense when they are not accepted.

From the beginning of Jesus' ministry, He called His men to follow Him and walk with Him. Jesus did this before He introduced

Two of the author's best friends. Marcel Turner (left) and Coltin Rohn. Both were pivotal to the growth of my early days in campus ministry. Marcel now leads one of the fastest-growing campus ministries in Miami, and Coltin leads the Columbus ICC.

doctrinal tenets of the faith. Since the disciples were already part of the family, so to speak, when Jesus introduced challenging concepts to them, they readily accepted them, having seen His lifestyle and trusting His love for them. We could create more volunteer opportunities, internships, and MERCY community service events to include students who are not disciples. Students, more than ever, are looking to be involved in events they feel can make an impact in their community. They want to be hands-on, whether it is helping the poor, the environment, or those undergoing oppression. There is a massive opportunity for the church to build its campus ministry through such events.

WORSHIP EXPERIENCE

The post-truth culture values experience more than truth. One of the most vital elements of our fellowship is our singing. I love the acapella singing and how everyone sings with all their heart. Visitors are blown away by this, as in most other churches' worship there is a loud band, and the words of the songs can be shallow. Jesus says we are to worship in spirit and truth. (**John 4:23-24**) I do not think it would be too much to say that this generation values worship in spirit more than truth. We can never get away from the pure-hearted worship, singing with our voices to God. At the same time, our churches need to become all things to all people. The strength of some denominational songs is that they emphasize experience and emotion. Including one or two contemporary Christian songs into our worship will help those in this generation connect to God in our services and devotionals. We should accommodate our worship services to meet this increasing need so they will want to study the Bible for the truth.

In 2015, Microsoft did a study on attention spans and found them to be shrinking to less than that of a goldfish.[17] This increasing short attention span should not be surprising considering our fast-paced and social-media-based society. Could it be that a 45-minute sermon might do more to push someone away than a 30-minute sermon that is focused on one call to action from the Bible?

One of my best friends, Marcel Turner, has recently found success in having weekly additions at his campus ministry at FIU in Miami. When I asked what he thinks has been the primary contributor to their growth, I was surprised to find that he shortened his sermons at devotionals with the focus more on the experience. More than ever, students desire to have community, food, fellowship, and fun. His devotionals involve dancing, activities, food, and a spiritual party of sorts! Marcel strives to strike the emotion and give the students an experience. No wonder he has taken a small group of seven to over 100 in his campus ministry in 18 months. Indeed, these concepts remind us of the early church. (**Acts 2:42-47**)

At one point, one of the largest and most famous churches in NYC, Hillsong, had grown and attracted even celebrities to their church. People love the worship experience and the emotional peak that their worship experience creates. The church is not grounded in truth, and the result is no true discipleship or life change. Yet, could not we as disciples of Jesus Christ learn from these churches' success by implementing strategies to make the gospel attractive in our worship services? Are we providing an experience to which college

---

17 Kevin McSpadden, "You Now Have a Shorter Attention Span than a Goldfish," *Time*, May 14, 2015, https://time.com/3858309/attention-spans-goldfish/.

students are drawn, which will, in turn, make them want to study the Bible?

We can never lower the standard of God's Word, but we may have to consider our approach to reaching a future generation as the post-truth shift continues to blur the lines of what is right and wrong. I have simply just offered some thoughts here to get us thinking if there are changes we can make in our church culture that will contribute to the goal we desire to see: Campus students baptized for Christ as true disciples with hard-lined convictions. Let us pray that the Holy Spirit continues to guide God's movement to evangelize the world in our generation through our campus ministries.

How Bad Do You Want It?

JESUS PAID the ultimate price for world evangelism by giving up His life. To Jesus, no cost was too great for the mission of God to be accomplished. How about you? Are you ready to sacrifice your time, energy, finances, and comfort to live the life of a campus leader? I hope that this book will serve as a valuable tool to lead your campus ministry to victory. The concepts are nothing new. Our brother Paul was already doing them there in Ephesus. The question must come, how badly do you want to build an excellent campus ministry?

We talk about wanting campus ministries of thousands of students but are you willing to share your faith with thousands? Nothing can replace a desire and passion! Napoleon Hill, author of the top-selling book *Think and Grow Rich,* said, "The starting point of all achievement is desire." For the disciple of Jesus, this desire must be ignited by the Holy Spirit. Jeremiah says it nicely, *"But if I say, 'I will not mention His Word or speak anymore in His name,' His Word is in my heart like a fire, a fire shut up in my bones. I am weary of holding it in; indeed, I cannot."* **(Jeremiah 20:9)** If you read all of **Jeremiah 20:7-18**, you will find Jeremiah did not want to proclaim God's message because of the hardship he had endured. Though he was feeling a lot, there was an inner fire that he could not hold in. How bad did he want it? The fire inside him made him willing to pay any price that would come his way.

The world is currently more confused than ever before. Campus leaders are the ones who will bring hope to the next generation. If you are reading this book, God has chosen you to be a part of a Holy Spirit-led generation of unencumbered, idealistic college students bent on changing the world for Christ! The hope of the future of God's modern-day movement and Christianity, in general, hangs on the campus ministry. Church, let us now more than ever be laser-focused on our campus ministries and commit ourselves to evangelize our campuses and thus the world in our generation. Decide today to begin *Project Tyrannus* at your college campus! To God be all the glory.

Living in the Book of Acts

*An Apology for the SoldOut Movement's Five
Core Distinguishing Convictions*

IF WE WANT BIBLE results, it is going to take Bible effort. The truth is many campus ministries have moments of fire for God and experience growth that quickly fades away or reaches a cap. The lukewarmness comes largely due to these ministries existing in autonomous churches. In an autonomous church, the campus students can only have an impact on their local congregation. The glory of being in a global movement is that the campus students can be raised up to have a global impact! Only in a global movement of churches that strive to follow the first-century church's paradigm and leadership convictions found in the Bible can a campus ministry genuinely thrive. It is crucial in our day when there is so much false teaching that our college students understand the five core convictions of the SoldOut Movement. These essentially biblical concepts must be continually restored and practiced in each successive generation for all nations to be evangelized.

"Core" is defined as the central or most important part of something, while "conviction" is a firmly held belief or opinion. It should be said that these are not the core convictions of the Christian faith (the deity and incarnation of Christ, salvation is by grace through faith, etc.), but the core convictions of the SoldOut Movement. The Christian faith's core convictions are what every baptized disciple in the movement studies in the Bible as outlined in our First Principles study series. The result is their salvation! We believe anyone who hears the message of Christ (**Romans 10:17**), believes the gospel (**John 3:16**), repents of their sin, decides to be a disciple (**Acts 2:38; Matthew 28:18-20**), is baptized (**1 Peter 3:21**), and is part of a fellowship that teaches these essential truths (**Acts 2:41-42**) is saved regardless of what the name of their fellowship is. Therefore, believing and holding to the SoldOut Movement's Five Core Convictions is an issue of proclamation and not one of salvation (although these can have implications that affect salvation, i.e., lukewarmness, unwillingness to speak the truth in love, etc.). The most effective way our campus ministries can participate and impact Jesus' dream of world evangelism is by knowing, holding to, and living out these core convictions.

The Five Core Convictions of the SoldOut Movement are:

1. We are a Bible church, not just a New Testament church.
2. We speak where the Bible is silent and stay silent where the Bible speaks.
3. The church is composed of sold-out disciples through discipling relationships.

4. A central leader and central leadership.
5. The evangelization of the nations in one generation.

Be a Bible church, not just a New Testament church!

The Apostles understood that the law (the Old Testament) was the Scriptures for the first-century church. If you lived when the Book of Acts was written, the Old Testament was your Bible! The sacrifice of Christ took away the Mosaic Law (sacrificing animals, temple worship, etc.), and yet you would know the Old Testament could be referenced or used in your discipleship. Paul wrote concerning the Old Testament to the evangelist Timothy, *"All Scripture is God-breathed and is useful for teaching, rebuking, correcting and training in righteousness, so that the servant of God may be thoroughly equipped for every good work."* (**2 Timothy 3:16-17**) "Scripture" in this pre-canonical context referred to the Old Testament. By extension it, of course, refers now to the New Testament, but Paul was encouraging Timothy, a church leader whom he was discipling, to use the Old Testament to teach, correct, rebuke, and train the church. The physical nation of Israel foreshadowed spiritual Israel, which is God's church. The Old Testament contains physical realities of spiritual truths. What is said about the leadership structure in the Book of Acts is less important because the Old Testament was the Bible for the early church. Teachings on the leadership paradigm for the early Christian church were already in their Bible. The plea to "restore the New Testament church" is therefore misleading if not understood in a theologically correct way. We are to be a Bible church.

Speak where the Bible is silent; be silent where the Bible speaks!

Many of our detractors and those who have left the faith challenge the movement's convictions, yet none offer "a better way" to evangelize the world than what the Scriptures say. Some have even claimed it is unbiblical to teach we are to evangelize the world in a generation. One former evangelist's challenge to us was to read the Book of Acts and see if we find the SoldOut Movement's Five Core Convictions in that book; he boldly claims they are not present. The logic behind this statement is deeply flawed for many reasons. It assumes that if something is not in the Bible or emphasized, it is inherently wrong. I believe such conclusions are drawn from past hurts and a lack proper biblical exegesis. If a youth minister hurt me, I may come to a conviction that the church should not have a youth minister. I could boldly challenge you to read the Book of Acts and say, "Look for a youth minister; you will not find it!" The fallacy of this logic becomes apparent immediately. There are many things you would not find in the Book of Acts. It could also be argued that "Campus Ministry" is not in the Bible.

Consider this quote on the book of Acts from Gordon Fee and Douglas Stuart's book *How to Read the Bible for All It's Worth:*

> The crucial hermeneutical question here is whether biblical narratives that describe what *happened* in the early church also function as norms intended to delineate *what should or must happen* in the ongoing church. Are there instances from Acts in which one may appropriately say, "We *must* do this," or should one merely say, "We *may* do this"? Our assumption, shared by many others, is this: *Unless Scripture*

explicitly tells us we must do something, what is only nar-
rated or described does not function in a normative (i.e.,
obligatory) way—unless it can be demonstrated on other
grounds that the author intended it to function in this way.[18]

I agree here with Fee and Stuart that patterns in the Bible are not binding and that commands are always binding. The Mainline Church of
Christ (MCOC), where the SoldOut Movement can trace its roots, is
deeply rooted in its "restoration" mentality. It is clear from the introduction to this book how their theology helped kill their campus
ministry growth. Growing up in the International Church of Christ
(ICOC), where I became a disciple and received my Bachelor's
degree in Biblical Studies from Oklahoma Christian University (at
the former extension campus named Cascade in Portland, Oregon),
a Mainline Church of Christ college, I loved the idea of "restoring the
first-century church." However, after seeing the fruit of this thinking and how it was implemented in the Mainline Church and now
the ICOC, I believe this "restoration" mentality, although noble, can
hurt us theologically if not understood properly. Certainly, we want
to be the church of the Bible that Jesus started, (**Matthew 16:13-19**)
and, in that sense, restore it in its obedience to God's commands!
Yet when the *example* of the early church found in Acts becomes
binding law, we can miss the author Luke's purpose and what he
meant to show us. (**2 Corinthians 3:6**)

The Mainline Church of Christ's mode of Bible interpretation that
Thomas Campbell coined was "to speak where the Bible speaks and
be silent where the Bible is silent." This phrase was twisted to mean

---

18   G. Fee, & D. Stuart, *How to Read the Bible for All It's Worth* (Zondervan, 2003), 124.

that if the Bible says something, we have the authority to do it, but it must be forbidden if the Bible is silent. This slogan has led to legalism and the forbidding of musical instruments, women baptizing, etc. There had to be a command, example, or inference to do something in the church. I remember being in Boston and talking to a Mainline Church of Christ preacher about the possibility of his joining us. He could not get over the fact that I thought it was acceptable to use church money to put on a devotional at a bowling alley. "Where is the money used to do that in the Bible?" he said. Many with this thinking espouse ideas, such as only meeting in houses for service, only taking benevolence-type collections, and in extreme cases, not celebrating holidays. Their challenge to us is, "Where is that found in the Book of Acts?" With this theology, they would be correct in many instances, but they face many challenges. How far do you go with this thinking? Does a true Christian need to dress the same way the early Christians did? Does a church service need to go through midnight? (**Acts 20:7-12**) Do we need to put money at the church leader's feet instead of in a basket or plate? (**Acts 4:37**) Certainly, these things are not wrong, but are they necessary? How far do you go "restoring" the book of Acts? This type of theology has been the most divisive, and even those who think like this cannot agree on how much is to be "restored." It is a black-hole *letter of the law* theology that leaves the soul empty and looking for the *life of the Spirit.* (**2 Corinthians 3:6; Galatians 3:1-14**)

A dear friend of mine, who left the SoldOut Movement, asked me if church leaders can give commands from the pulpit that are opinions and not Scripture. Is this not what is done every Sunday in any church when the week's announcements are given? An announcement is made that the Midweek service is going to be Wednesday at 7:30 PM. The time a church meets is an opinion and not a biblical mandate. As a campus minister, you will give much direction to guide the ministry that does not come directly from the Bible. **Hebrews 13:17** is in the Bible for this very reason. *"Obey your leaders and submit to their authority. They keep watch over you as men who must give an account. Obey them so that their work will be a joy and not a burden for that would be of no advantage to you."* Biblically, leadership has the authority to speak where the Bible is silent.

Leaders bring unity and direction to God's people. This is such a freeing thought for campus leaders! You can use your creativity and innovation to help direct God's people. A lot of ministry is not necessarily right versus wrong, but sometimes good, better, or best. Leaders must speak where the Bible is silent for the congregation, or there will be disorder and chaos. (**1 Corinthians 14:33**) In a family, the father would be wise to solicit input from the members, but ultimately, he is responsible for deciding what is and isn't best in any given situation. This same type of decision-making was done in the early church by James, who spoke where the New Covenant was silent, if you will, by commanding the whole movement to abstain from food polluted by idols with feedback from the Jerusalem elders and Peter. (**Acts 15:19-21**) Of note, James' decision was based on scriptural principles as he references both Isaiah and Amos! It was made authoritative in the form of a letter, and the letter was circulated to the churches for them to obey. (**Acts 16:4**)

To speak where the Bible is silent is part of the glory of our freedom in Christ. God, in his genius, understands that every culture and generation is different, so, of course, examples in Scripture couldn't be exclusively binding. A certain way the church did things in Acts may not be the best way in today's culture. In some cases, it may be. An inquisitive, quick reading through the book of Acts will show the leadership structure changed and molded according to the needs, as they were free to speak where the law was silent. We are free to choose how to do missions, spend money as a movement, structure our ministries, etc. The book of Acts is then not a book prescribing church polity or structure, but a book showing how the flexibility in which the first-century disciples lived led to the miraculous, geographical expansion of the church, as the Spirit moved the disciples to evangelize the world in their lifetime.

If the Bible commands something, we are to be silent and obey what God says. Where it is silent, we have the freedom to come up with methodologies that can be implemented prayerfully, based on biblical principles that propagate God's purposes. Use this God-given freedom to come up with campaigns, events, meetings, roles, etc., that forcefully advance your campus ministry. In retrospect, we must instead be silent where the Bible speaks and speak where the Bible is silent. This heart of obedience toward God's commands will always bear the fruit of proper biblical restoration.

Build the church with sold-out disciples who thrive on discipling relationships!

Every baptized disciple has given up everything to follow Jesus. (**Matthew 13:44-45; Luke 14:25-33**) After one is baptized, that new disciple is commanded to be taught to obey Jesus' commands by another disciple. (**Matthew 28:20**) There are around 59 "one another" verses in the Bible, including *"love one another,"* (**John 13:34-35**), *"confess your sins to one another,"* (**James 5:16**) and *"carry each other's* *burdens." (**Galatians 6:2**). To obey Jesus' command and fulfill the "one another" passages, the SoldOut Movement's leadership has decided that every Christian will have a discipling partner to encourage them in their walk with God. Just like churches are not autonomous and need an outside authority to help guide and encourage one another, so do Christians. They need others to disciple them.

Where does one find "discipleship partners" and "Bible Talk leaders" in the Book of Acts? Did potential baptisms need to "count the cost" before getting baptized? The gospel of Luke is a narrative that contains the teachings of discipleship and what it means to be "sold out" to God. (**Acts 1:1**) The Book of Acts is a narrative of the results of those very teachings! We are not privy to all the information covered when, for example, Philip studied the word with the Ethiopian eunuch. (**Acts 8:29-36**) We can assume that Philip reviewed the teachings of Jesus that Luke covered in his gospel. (**Acts 1:1**) Jesus commanded that everyone count the cost before their baptism, (**Luke 9:57-62; 14:25-33**) and certainly the eunuch did this, or Philip would not have baptized him.

Those who oppose the idea of a standard of mentoring across a movement of churches have argumentatively asked, "Who discipled the Ethiopian eunuch?" Similar sentiments are given when they bring up church history, which says the Ethiopian eunuch started the church in Ethiopia without any direction or outside authority. Scripture will not contradict Scripture. If this tradition is accurate, we can assume the eunuch went back to the Jerusalem Church, or one of the churches started after the dispersion of the Christians in **Acts 8:1-4**. He could have been a part of the church, trained, and eventually sent off to Ethiopia, commissioned by the church through the Holy Spirit.

The early church account in Acts in its unadulterated beginnings was completely sold out to Christ. The 3,000 baptized in **Acts 2:41** were indistinguishable from the 120 waiting in prayerfulness in Acts 1, who were indistinguishable from the original 12, who were indistinguishable from Jesus Christ! Discipling is the only way to reach the ends of the earth. Someone once said it is the glue of the movement. Looking at the SoldOut Movement's Five Core Convictions under the light of the Word of God, it is strange to think many would not accept these teachings. We cannot be deceived; the root issue is not the teachings that form the basis of these convictions but the heart of the men and women who oppose them.

We have seen so many miracles, but many of us have had friends and even a few fallen evangelists who have renounced the SoldOut Movement's Five Core Convictions and left the church. The truth is that being a part of a movement takes incredible sacrifice. The convictions themselves require us to practice the qualities that please God: Humility, faith, submission, and trust. Unsurprisingly, we are more susceptible to being hurt by fellow disciples in the true church of God because we have family-level openness and vulnerability with one another, unlike most churches where many members only attend on Sunday. In every case that a leader has left the movement, I have noticed the determining factor has boiled down to them not getting what they wanted. Whether it was a leadership position they desired, or whether they were asked to send people to another church, or whether they felt that the Special Missions contribution multiple was too much, it all came down to them having to give up something.

I do not look down òn these fallen men and women, as they simply gave into the sins that are so common to men. It should be a sober reminder for all of us as disciples to stay humble. I am not a part of the central leadership of the SoldOut Movement; the World Sector Leaders group or Crown of Thorns Council. I am an evangelist called by God, living my dream of preaching the gospel. I have led two churches and had to send out many to support other churches or church plantings. Having to send out some of your top leaders can be tough when the church is still small. Of course, when such calls from God come, autonomy and a rejection of the Five Core Convictions appeal to the leader and disciple who is not close to God or disconnected from the mission—Satan knows how and when to strike! Many times, it is not even the church that struggles. They understand disciples are sold out to Jesus. It is often the leaders of the church who struggle. What kept my wife, Chenelle, and me surrendered in the face of such constant sacrifice? Through so much discipling from Matt and Helen Sullivan, who oversaw the church in Gainesville, I learned that God would provide no matter what was asked! The Orlando Church they led had only been around a little over three years when we were in Gainesville, and they planted both Gainesville and Houston, sending their top leaders. Yet, God has taken care of them as they still grew to over 100 disciples and planted the church in Miami by sending out half the church! We experienced first-hand how we were all part of one global church. *"It is more blessed to give than to receive,"* the Lord said. (**Acts 20:35**) There is no cost too high financially or physically that God could ask us for the salvation of just one soul. In the end, it is Jesus' example of submitting to God, even to the point of death that inspires us to keep discipling and being discipled.

Bottom line, some leaders who have left God's movement simply did not get what they wanted and then changed their "convictions" to appease their conscience and validate their desires that were supposed to be given up at baptism. An evangelist who is not experiencing numerical growth may decide to compromise his conviction by not baptizing disciples anymore. (**John 4:1-2**) He now does not feel people need to "jump through so many hoops" to be baptized. A church leader who does not want to give up someone to another church can be tempted to begin questioning central leadership because autonomy becomes even more appealing. Another leader may tire of the financial sacrifice to support foreign missionaries, and so, once again, autonomy becomes the forbidden fruit. This lack of submission leads to a bitterness towards God's movement that defiles many as they publicly criticize it while shipwrecking the faith of the unstable. (**Hebrews 12:15**) It shipwrecks those who listen because their pleas appeal to the sinful nature not to have to be surrendered to God. Peter talks about false teachers and their motivations. "With eyes full of adultery, they never stop sinning; they seduce the unstable; they are experts in greed —an accursed brood… For they mouth empty, boastful words and, by appealing to the lustful desires of the flesh, they entice people who are just escaping from those who live in error." (**2 Peter 2:14, 18**) This bitterness drives people into believing strange doctrines in their attempt to distance themselves from the movement's theology. Our prayer is that many of our fallen brothers and sisters will return to these biblical convictions and join us in evangelizing the nations in our generation.

Institute a central leadership with a central leader!

Reading the Book of Acts will reveal that the churches worked together and were not locally autonomous (self-governing) congregations. They shared money to support staff (**Acts 18:5**) and met benevolent needs. (**Acts 11:29-30**) **Acts 15** reveals a central leadership that governed and preserved unity in the worldwide church.

God's SoldOut Movement is structured with a central leader (currently Dr. Kip McKean) and a central leadership (the World Sector Leaders and Crown of Thorns Council). Is there biblical precedence for this structure? Before we delve into this issue, I want to remind us that this question assumes there *must be* biblical precedence for a leadership structure, which, as argued earlier, is not necessarily the case. We do believe, though, that where the Bible is silent, we should do our best to base what we believe on scriptural principles and the spirit of Scripture. Yet, as you dig deep into your Bible, I believe you will find much biblical precedence for this leadership structure. Though Acts is not a book on church polity, you will find clues for how the church functioned. Before we do, let us go back to the Old Testament and see what those living in the Book of Acts would have read in their Bibles (Old Testament) concerning the need for leadership and structure. Here are a few passages to consider:

Listen now to me and I will give you some advice, and may God be with you. You must be the people's representative before God and bring their disputes to him. Teach them His decrees and instructions, and show them the way they are to live and how they are to behave. But select capable men from all the people—men who fear God, trustworthy men who hate dishonest gain—and appoint them as officials over thousands, hundreds, fifties and tens. Have them serve as judges for the people at all times, but have them bring every difficult case to you; the simple cases they can decide themselves. That will make your load lighter, because they will share it with you. If you do this and God so commands, you will be able to stand the strain, and all these people will go home satisfied.

-EXODUS 18:19-23

Moses said to the Lord, "May the Lord, the God who gives breath to all living things, appoint someone over this community to go out and come in before them, one who will lead them out and bring them in, so the Lord's people will not be like sheep without a shepherd.

-NUMBERS 27:15-17

God commanded Moses to lead the people and appoint men who feared God to lead thousands, hundreds, fifties, and tens. Moses was the central leader, and those men would form the central leadership. Moses was then to make sure that there would be a central leader after he passed (Joshua) so the people would not be like sheep without a shepherd. In the New Testament, Paul sent an evangelist (Timothy) into a church, as he oversaw that congregation he planted. (**1 Corinthians 4:14-17**) This ability and authority established the *"same teaching everywhere in every church."* (**1 Corinthians 4:17**) Titus was the overseeing evangelist (historically called "bishop") of Crete and was told by Paul to appoint shepherds in every church in Crete. (**Titus 1:5**)

The early Christians understood that anytime God's people were united and prospering, there was a central leader (i.e., Moses, Joshua, David, Jesus, and the Apostles, etc.). Central leadership is at the very core unit of the human family. We can agree that the father is the central leader of the family (or is supposed to be!); businesses have CEOs and bosses; and sports teams always have coaches. Most autonomous churches believe in one-man leadership to some degree (they have a pastor or lead evangelist). Yet, the logical fallacy is that they do not believe in it for a worldwide movement or family of churches.

Fear cannot motivate us to compromise biblical commands and principles. It is sad when a wife experiences an abusive husband, but that does not mean the problem is with marriage structure, but rather the sin in that man's life. A godly husband will solicit input from his wife and children, delegate responsibilities to them, and choose to submit to their wisdom at times, yet he will make the final decision.

I am so grateful for how Dr. Kip McKean has led God's SoldOut Movement through grace and truth since 2006. I had the opportunity to be discipled by Kip and experience the building of this incredible family of churches. It is Kip's vision that has fueled our fellowship to have a campus ministry focus. I have seen Kip regularly take corrections and solicit input. He has always apologized and owned up to mistakes he has made, and at the same time, he boldly recognizes his call to lead God's people. It should be said that we do not believe in a "Pope"—a central leader who stands above God's Word—but rather, we believe in a leader who submits himself to God's Word and the needs of God's people. Even in the Jerusalem Council meeting of **Acts 15**, the central leadership displayed incredible humility deferring to God's Word on the subject they were discussing. Kip has said countless times in sermons he has preached that he "does not hear the audible voice of God" but, like all of us, strives his best to live as Jesus did and hear His voice through Scripture. Personally, I have never met anyone who is as close to Jesus in their example, in the grace he shows, in the discipline of his life, and his vision to win the world. As Jesus said, whoever wants to be great must be a slave of all, and I believe this is why Kip is leading our movement. God always determines his leadership. (**Acts 20:28; Ephesians 4:11-13**)

The question inevitably always comes: Who was the one-man leader in the New Testament? Our detractors want a point-blank verse from the Book of Acts that says something like "Peter was the leader of God's entire movement." They are unwilling to submit to the Old Testament's abundantly clear passages because of their "New Testament only" theology that disallows God's creative structures, principles, and paradigms lived out by His people in the Old Testament to become authoritative and directive in the lives of His people living as the Body of Christ under the New Covenant. This interpretation comes from insufficient theology based on a humanistic interpretation of "be silent where the Bible is silent" (for them—where the New Testament is silent). The most obvious example of one-man leadership is in Jesus Christ, who founded the church. (**Matthew 16:13-19**) I will attempt to answer the question of who led the first-century movement, even though scripturally, this is not the purpose of either the gospels or Acts since they were built upon the Old Testament foundation. The fact that Jesus was one man, whom we are called to imitate, should be enough of an example for us as a church today to believe in one-man leadership.

I believe that Peter was the leader of God's first-century church movement after Jesus ascended to heaven. The fact that Catholics believe Peter was the first Pope should not be dismissed so quickly by Protestants. The doctrine of apostolic succession is unscriptural, of course, but it should cause us to pause for a moment to figure out why Peter was viewed as the leader of the whole church early in its history.

Unfortunately, the Mainline Church of Christ so reacted to the Catholic's false doctrine that they decided autonomy was the guiding principle of church government. Their reactionary theology kept them from searching the Scriptures for a biblical model of church structure. Peter, or any successive central leader, was not above Scripture, as the Catholics teach, and cannot make doctrine for the church since Jesus and His word are the foundation. (**Ephesians 2:18-20**) Consider these facts from Scripture that support the view that Jesus chose him to be the central leader for the first-century movement:

- Peter is always listed first in the list of Apostles. (**Matthew 10:1-4—** "first" is used in referring to Peter; **Mark 3:16-19; Luke 6:14-16; Acts 1:13**)
- Peter usually spoke on behalf of the Apostles. (**Luke 9:32; Luke 12:41; John 6:68-69**)
- Jesus said it would be Peter's faith that would strengthen the brothers. (**Luke 22:32**)
- The resurrected Jesus asked Peter, "Do you love me more than these?" (Referring to the other Apostles by some scholars). He then proceeded to tell him to feed His sheep. Peter was to feed all of Jesus' sheep, to shepherd Jesus' people! (**John 21:15-17**)
- Peter led the meeting to replace Judas with Matthias. (**Acts 1:15-26**)
- Peter was given the keys to the kingdom, and this is fulfilled when he preached the first gospel message at Pentecost. (**Matthew 16:13-19; Acts 2:36-42**)
- It was Peter who received the revelation to allow the Gentiles to accept the gospel. (**Acts 10-11**)
- Jesus appeared first to Peter and then to *the twelve.* (**1 Corinthians 15:5**)

- Jesus addressed Peter when the disciples fell asleep on him and not the whole group. (**Mark 14:37-38**)

In **Acts 15**, Luke chronicles the Jerusalem Council, where the early church's central leadership (the Apostles and elders) came together to discuss a potentially movement-ending controversy. Some Jews were teaching one must be circumcised to be saved, and a meeting was called to resolve the issue by the Jerusalem church. James (the brother of Jesus) led the Jerusalem church and made the final verdict (**Acts 15:19**). What happened to Peter as the leader? Is it possible James was leading the early church movement at this point? Although things get a little unclear, might I present an alternative view?

My conviction is that Peter stopped leading the Jerusalem church when he was miraculously delivered from prison and fled to *"another place."*

> *"Peter motioned with his hand for them to be quiet and described how the Lord had brought him out of prison. 'Tell James and the other brothers and sisters about this,' he said, and then he left for another place."* (**Acts 12:17**)

We can assume Peter put James in charge of the Jerusalem church. He possibly was placed in charge of the movement, but I believe Peter still led the entire movement even after this point. A careful reading of **Acts 15** reveals Peter came back to Jerusalem for the council meeting, and it could be argued that he leads the council meeting. Peter is the one who stands up and addresses the council after some beginning discussion. (**Acts 15:6**) When James speaks up, he defers to what Peter ("Simon") says as the authority. (**Acts 15:14**) James then simply expresses his judgment, resulting in a letter written for all the churches to obey. Peter is later called an elder and mentions Jesus being the "Chief Shepherd." (**1 Peter 5:1-4**)

A modern parallel is our current structure in the fellowship of churches that I serve. Kip McKean, who serves as our central leader, commissioned Tim and Lianne Kernan to lead the City of Angels ICC (LA church), which he previously led so he and his wife Elena could focus exclusively on his missionary travels to strengthen and start churches—this is likely what Peter did when he left Jerusalem. Kip left Tim Kernan in charge (like Peter left James) of the Los Angeles church. It would be fitting that if there is a Central Leadership Council meeting in LA that Tim would host the group and defer to Kip's decision in his final judgment since Kip still leads the whole movement. History says that Peter went on to lead the church in Rome (called "Babylon" figuratively in **1 Peter 5:13**), which naturally became the spiritual center of influence for the entire first-century movement of God since Rome was the lead city of the secular Roman Empire. It should not surprise us then that the early church saw Peter as the overall leader, and sadly, with the false doctrine of the third century, eventually the Pope. Just because they twisted his role does not mean we should do away with "one-man central leadership" taught clearly in the Old Testament, and now we see practiced even in the New Testament.

Leadership is of God, and it is to be obeyed in the churches. (**Hebrews 13:17**) Leadership must speak with God-given authority where the Bible is silent, in areas that provide unity and direction for the church. It should go without being said—you do not obey a leader who calls you to go against biblical commands. Regardless of whether the first-century church's central leader was Peter or James, it is clear that one man decided with a healthy amount of discussion and feedback on the issue of Gentile requirements for being Christians for the entire movement of churches. The final decision was drafted into a letter to be carried out for all the churches to obey. (Acts 16:4-5) Leadership teaches and preaches the Bible with all authority and expects people to obey, which is done through humility, love, patience, and faith.

Special Missions contribution is an amazing concept our leadership has come up with to fulfill Jesus' dream to evangelize the world by planting churches. Campus students are called to work hard to raise money for missions in our fellowship because of their youth and vigor. A call is put out once or twice a year for disciples to give a "multiple" of their weekly contributions to support mission work planned worldwide for the calendar year. Some have said this puts too much pressure on the churches and ask why Christians cannot just meet in homes as they did in the Book of Acts while not paying their preachers.

The question must be raised of why they met in homes in the Book of Acts. Did they have access to hotel rental spaces such as we do? Maybe they did not think of it since Christianity started as a house church movement. Maybe they did meet in places besides homes (Acts 19—see the Lecture Hall of Tyrannus and the temple courts in Acts 2:42-27). My point is the leadership chose to do it a certain way, and the people were behind them. Would God not want us to use the resources we have to accomplish His mission (Ephesians 5:16) today? Jesus said you must judge a tree by its fruit. (Luke 6:44) Sadly, our detractors who have so loudly proclaimed a "return to New Testament Christianity" through the meeting in homes exclusively, not paying ministers, no central leadership, etc., yet have had minimal impact and ARE NOT living out the Book of Acts, as evidenced by their lack of geographic expansion.

By contrast, the SoldOut Movement has expanded to every populated continent of the world in the last eleven years. There is nothing wrong with meeting in homes or not having full-time staff. Still, we have decided as a leadership that the fastest way to accomplish the mission of Christ is to imitate the example of Jesus. He had a full-time staff (**Mark 1:14-20; Luke 10**) and we have invested most of our money into starting and maintaining new churches and their leadership. (**1 Corinthians 9:14**) Praise God for churches who have been brought to unity by the blood of Jesus and a central leader and central leadership to share our resources to build a worldwide church to the glory of our great God.

This great doctrine and conviction being restored in our day have allowed us to mobilize college students worldwide to do great things for God. It allows campus students to have a global family that they can connect with on social media. The students can take brothers and sisters out on dates from other churches or fellowship at conferences, having more options of whom to date and marry. The list could go on of all the benefits of a central leadership for the campus ministries. Perhaps the most important is if a campus ministry or church is struggling or drifting into lukewarmness, the overseeing evangelist can come in and help strengthen them, or in some cases, make leadership changes that benefit the entire church. This structure is one of the many reasons our fellowship remains sold out to God. A central leader and central leadership give our congregations a unified vision and shared resources to see the world evangelized in this generation.

Evangelize the nations in one generation!

The theological purpose of the Book of Acts is outlined in the beginning by Luke in Acts, *"But you will receive power when the Holy Spirit comes on you; and you will be my witnesses in Jerusalem, and in all Judea and Samaria, and to the ends of the earth."* (**Acts 1:8**) Acts chronicles the early movement's expansion to the ends of the earth: **Acts 1-7** (Jerusalem-Judea), **Acts 8** (Samaria), and **Acts 9-28** (ends of the earth/Gentile nations). Luke's intention is to show how a Jewish-based community became a worldwide Gentile movement by the power of the Spirit.

We are to evangelize the world in this generation. Evangelizing the world does not mean everyone will become a disciple, but that everyone gets the chance to become one by encountering God's church and hearing the message. Campus ministry is the fastest way to do this, but if our students do not understand this conviction, the urgency will not be present in your ministry. This was the command of Jesus to the 11 faithful disciples, *"Therefore, go and make disciples of all nations, baptizing them in the name of the Father, the Son, and the Holy Spirit."* (**Matthew 28:19**) Jesus commanded those eleven to get to all nations. How could they unless they did it before they died (their generation)? A recent analogy that Lead Evangelist of the City of Angels ICC, Tim Kernan, used at a staff meeting demonstrates this point. If I am a parent and tell my kids to make their bed and clean their room, would it not be foolish if they questioned if I meant in their generation? Of course, it means in their lifetime! I am astonished that anyone would think such a noble vision is unbiblical. The only time those 11 Apostles could get to all nations was in their generation. Then Jesus commands them to teach those they baptize to obey everything He taught, including to go to all nations! I believe that someone who fights against this vision from Jesus to evangelize the world in our generation is extremely far from God, and something is going on in their heart.

In His Olivet discourse, Jesus said, *"And this gospel of the kingdom will be preached in the whole world as a testimony to all nations, and then the end will come."* (**Matthew 24:14**) "The end" refers to the destruction of the temple by the Roman general Titus that would occur in 70 AD. (**Matthew 24:1-2**) Jesus taught the world was going to be evangelized in their generation before the temple was destroyed. Luke uses **Acts 1:8** to reiterate Jesus' command and chronicles the church from its beginning in 29 AD to accomplishing its expansion to the ends of the earth. While on house arrest, Paul would later write around 61 AD from Rome to the disciples in Colosse, *"This is the gospel that you heard and that has been proclaimed to every creature under heaven, and of which I, Paul, have become a servant."* (**Colossians 1:23**) They accomplished the evangelization of the known world in their generation, and later in 70 AD, the temple would be destroyed, fulfilling Jesus' words.

After Jesus' commission to go into all nations, He told His 11 faithful Apostles, with their newly baptized disciples, to be *"teaching them to obey everything I have taught you."* (**Matthew 28:20**) Matthew certainly remembered Jesus' expectation of complete obedience to this global vision to disciple the nations! The conviction of urgency to get the job done in a generation now is emphasized again because some have thought that we should invest in the generations ahead of us. Some have mistakenly put the focus on merely teaching one's children to reach future generations. As noble as this sounds, what are we teaching our children if they do not see their parent's generation being won for Christ? The succeeding generations will simply imitate the lack of urgency of their fathers. Of course, Christ wants every future generation brought to Christ, but it requires us to be obedient to win *our* generation. This will not be accomplished without campus ministry!

Some have been concerned that evangelizing the nations in a generation puts too much pressure on disciples. This pressure is not from man but from God. The "message" of the Lord in the King James Version (KJV) of the Bible is often called the "burden" of the Lord (i.e., **Malachi 1:1** KJV). Every prophet in the Bible had an incredible amount of pressure on them from the message God gave them, which came at high personal costs. The world is lost, and the knowledge of its condition is an incredible weight we must carry as followers of Jesus. This burden, pressure, and weight should motivate us to make a difference.

If I came home to my apartment burning down and my wife was passed out inside, there would be a "pressure" or "burden" to run in and get her. This burden and risk is not an ungodly pressure, but a pressure motivated by love to rescue my wife from that burning building. The world is lost and burning in its sin, so we must embrace the pressure at an emotional, financial, or personal level to see the world evangelized. Paul was willing to suffer spiritually for this cause, (**Romans 9:1-4**) and was a man who *"face[d] daily the pressure of [his] concern for all the churches."* (**2 Corinthians 11:28**) If we are to be living in the Book of Acts, we must be a church that is a worldwide movement expanding to the ends of the earth and expecting to get the job of world evangelism done in our generation.

We now understand why it is essential as campus ministry leaders to know and teach these Five Distinguishing Core Convictions. We have seen from the Bible that the Book of Acts is a narrative showing the *results* of biblical convictions, not necessarily explaining the foundational *doctrines* in which they believed. Regardless, our brief survey of the Book of Acts did reveal plenty of examples of both. When these convictions are discipled into our campus students, they will be like the Bereans in Acts 17—noble-hearted towards the truth, and thus ready and willing to serve God in any way that may be asked by the Spirit. It is my prayer that this appendix article helps our detractors reconsider their ways, but even more, that it strengthens the convictions of disciples all around the world, especially in God's SoldOut Movement campus ministries, to uphold God's Word by embracing and defending our movement's Five Distinguishing Core Convictions! To God be the glory.

APPENDIX II

STUDENT ORGANIZATION SAMPLE CONSTITUTION TO BECOME A CLUB

BELOW IS A SAMPLE constitution[19] for a "Christian Club" you may be required to have on your campus. Every college may vary on what is to be included in a constitution. This document is just a sample constitution of a club idea using "Boston University" as an example. The modifications necessary will vary from campus to campus and especially from country to country. We advise you to gather a great deal of information on the process from your student union before you start.

---

19 Credit must be given to Anthony Eckels, original founder of the Orlando ICC remnant group for the original outline that the author has modified.

Constitution of Global Christian Revolution (GCR)

ARTICLE I. NAME OF ORGANIZATION
The name of this organization is Global Christian Revolution. The organization will utilize the acronym GCR to refer to itself and in public materials.

ARTICLE II. PURPOSE STATEMENT
Section A. Purpose
GCR fosters student leadership and personal engagement by providing support and discussion groups and celebrates cultural and racial diversity through its emphasis on missionary work. We do this by a study of the Bible and different cultures, creating spaces for cultural celebration, promoting leadership development, and providing opportunities for faith, education, and reflection.

Section B. Goals
GCR uses the Bible, artistic expression, missionary history/work, and cultural education to inspire students to have strong faith, use their talents, and excel academically. This is done through our "Global Groups" and "GCR Devotional" meetings that give students a venue to perform their art, share their backgrounds, and discuss faith. This club essentially upholds the definition of 'art' in these meetings: "the quality, production, expression, or realm, according to aesthetic principles, of what is beautiful, appealing, or of more than ordinary significance" (dictionary.com). The emphasis on global culture and diversity makes it unique to all other "faith groups" currently on campus.

GCR employs a creative atmosphere where any aspiring student can hone their artistic talent and contribute to the creative arts and faith community. Everyone has an artist growing within them: By providing various professional artists from various artistic backgrounds, aspiring artists can discover their artistic talent and grow while being supported by their student peers. Everyone has a cultural background that can be shared to broaden our global perspective as Christians.

GCR honors the fact that God has given talents and culture to everyone. By providing the opportunity for growth and development for all students from any religious background, ethnicity, or nation, aspiring artists can honor God's gifts to them by contributing their artistic perspectives about various faith topics. GCR realizes that there are many Abrahamic faiths that can contribute and grow together, learning from one another in a creative artistic environment.

ARTICLE III. COMPLIANCE STATEMENT
Upon approval by the Department of Student Activities and Involvement, GCR shall be a registered student organization at Boston University. GCR shall comply with all local, state, and federal laws, as well as all Boston University regulations, policies, and procedures. Such compliance includes but is not limited to the University's regulations related to Non-Discrimination, Sexual Harassment (including sexual misconduct, dating violence, domestic violence, and stalking), Hazing, Commercial Activity, and Student Leader Eligibility.

ARTICLE IV. UNIVERSITY REGULATIONS
Section A. Non-Discrimination
GCR agrees that it will not discriminate based on race, creed, color, religion, age, disability, sex, sexual orientation, gender identity and

expression, marital status, national origin, political opinions or affiliations, genetic information, and veteran status as protected under the Vietnam Era Veterans' Readjustment Assistance Act.

Section B. Sexual Harassment

GCR agrees that it will not engage in any activity that is unwelcome conduct of sexual nature that creates a hostile environment.

Section C. Hazing

GCR agrees that it will not initiate, support, or encourage any events or situations that recklessly, by design, or intentionally endanger the mental or physical health or safety of a student for any purpose, including but not limited to initiation or admission into or affiliation with any student group or organization.

Section D. Responsibility to Report

Suppose this organization becomes aware of any such conduct described in this article. In that case, GCR will report it immediately to Student Activities and Involvement, the Director of Student Conduct and Conflict Resolution, or the University's Title IX Coordinator.

ARTICLE V. MEMBERSHIP

Membership in this organization is open to all enrolled students at Boston University. Non-enrolled students, spouses, faculty, and staff may be associate members; however, they may not vote or hold office. All members and associate members are free to leave and disassociate without fear of retribution, retaliation, or harassment.

ARTICLE VI. OFFICERS

Section A: Eligibility

Potential officers must meet the minimum eligibility requirements of active student membership (Article III and IV). All officers of the organization shall possess (at the time of election and during their term) at least the minimum requirements regarding enrollment hours, GPA, academic and disciplinary standing, and financial and disciplinary holds to serve in a leadership position, as stated. Officers who do not meet these requirements during their term shall be resigned or removed.

Section B: Titles and Duties

The officers of this organization shall include a President, Vice President, Treasurer, and Secretary. No officer will be permitted to hold more than one officer position at a time unless appointed to an interim position.

The President shall:

- Supervise and coordinate the activities of the organization.
- Preside over all meetings and call all meetings to order.
- Maintain communication with the Office of Student Involvement and ensure that all paperwork is current.
- Be one of three signers on financial documents.
- Be responsible for creating a budget at the beginning of each fall and spring semester in conjunction with the Treasurer.
- Ensure that all officers are familiar with this Constitution via a review to happen within one month of officer installation.
- Ensure that all officers are performing their duties as defined in this Constitution.

- Keep advisor informed of activities and functions of the organization.
- Be familiar with Boston University regulations.
- Provide all documents and records pertaining to their responsibilities to the newly elected President.
- Assign special projects to officers.

The Vice President shall:
- Assist the President in their duties.
- Assume the President's responsibilities in their absence.
- Coordinate all conferences.
- Keep accurate records of all meetings in the Secretary's absence.
- Plan and be responsible for all retreats and training of the organization.
- Perform an audit of all financial transactions of the organization once per semester.
- Provide all documents and records pertaining to their responsibilities to the newly elected Vice President.
- Assist in special projects as assigned by the President.

The Treasurer shall:
- Keep an accurate account of all funds received and expended.
- Present a budget report of deposits and expenditures to the membership at least once per month, and as requested by the President, Vice President, advisor, or Office of Student Involvement.
- Be one of three signers on financial documents.
- Be responsible for collecting dues and notifying members who are delinquent in their payments.
- Be responsible for creating a budget at the beginning of each fall and spring semester in conjunction with the President.

- Provide financial records sufficient to allow the Vice President to perform audits.
- Provide all documents and records pertaining to their responsibilities to the newly elected Treasurer.
- Assist in special projects as assigned by the President.

The Secretary shall:
- Notify members of meetings via e-mail and/or telephone at least 48 hours in advance.
- Keep accurate minutes and records of all meetings.
- Maintain an accurate list of members and their contact information.
- Prepare the organization's registration forms at the beginning of each semester and when there are changes in organizational information over the course of the semester.
- Take attendance at all meetings and maintain an attendance record.
- Prepare ballots for elections.
- Check eligibility for potential officers before annual elections.
- Keep a copy of the constitution, and it is available for members.
- Provide all documents and records pertaining to their responsibilities to the newly elected Secretary.
- Assist in special projects as assigned by the President.
- Shall be appointed by the Vice President.

Section C. Voting Rights
All officers shall retain voting rights; however, the President shall only vote in the case of a tie, with the exception of officer elections.

Section D. Term of Office
The length of the term of office shall be no longer than one year.

Section E. Recruitment
Recruitment shall take place throughout the year, and membership is open at all times.

Section F. Voting Rights
Only active student members are eligible to vote.

Section G. Revocation of Membership
Membership may be revoked without a mutual agreement for non-participation, misconduct, or violations of any provisions of the Constitution. The member will be notified in writing of the possible revocation at least 72 hours prior to the vote and will be allowed to address the organization to relate to members any relevant defense prior to the voting for removal. Membership can only be revoked upon a 2/3 affirmative vote of active student members.

Section H. Reinstatement of Membership
Membership may be reinstated after one full semester has passed. The former member may submit a request for reinstatement to the President. At the next membership meeting, the organization must vote on the reinstatement request. Membership may be reinstated by a 2/3 affirmative vote of the active student members.

ARTICLE VII. ELECTIONS
Section A: Announcement of Elections
At least one meeting prior, the President shall announce the date of the upcoming nominations and elections. They shall also state the eligibility criteria (as in Article VI, Section A). All active student members interested in running for office should bring written proof of eligibility to the nominations/elections meeting.

Section B: Nomination Process

The nomination of officers shall occur each academic year at the membership meeting held in March. One of the officers not running for office (preference determined by the order listed in Article VI, starting with the President) shall facilitate the nomination and election process at this meeting. If this is not possible, the facilitator will be selected by a majority vote of active student members.

Any active student member present may nominate someone or themselves for office by verbally nominating the individual during this procedure. However, the nominee must be considered eligible for an officer position (as defined in Article VI, Section A as verified by the Secretary). Absentee/proxy ballots are not permitted in the nomination process.

Section C: Election Process

The election of officers shall occur at the membership meeting held in March. The order of elections shall be President, Vice President, Treasurer, and Secretary. The organization may not proceed to the next officer's election until the current one has been resolved.

The nominated candidates for each office will be given a chance to address the organization to discuss their qualifications and why they should be elected to that office. Candidates will speak to the organization in alphabetical order by last name. Once each candidate for that office has had the opportunity to speak, all active student members present (minus the nominations/elections facilitator described in Section C above) will have the opportunity to vote by secret ballot. Absentee/proxy ballots are not permitted in the election process.

The nominations/elections facilitator will tabulate all votes immediately, in the presence of the organization. A candidate shall be elected by a majority of all votes cast by active student members. If no candidate receives a majority of votes, the top two candidates will immediately enter a run-off election. In the event of a tie, the nominations/elections facilitator shall cast a vote to break the tie.

The nominations/elections facilitator will announce the new officer and ask if any active student member contests the count. If no active student member contests the count, the new officer shall take office. If an active student member contests the count, each candidate may select an active student member to supervise the recount. The nominations/elections facilitator will immediately recount all votes in the presence of the elected representatives. Once an officer is confirmed, the organization will proceed to elections for the next officer.

Section D: Installation of Officers
Newly elected officers shall take office immediately following the membership meeting in April, and their term will end immediately following the membership meeting the following April. Current officers should assist in the transition and training of the officers—elect, from elections until installation. A change in officer information should be reported to the University within ten school days of installation.

Section E: Re-election
However, any officer may be re-elected; however, not for more than two consecutive terms in the same officer position. Officers cannot reappoint themselves for a subsequent term; they must be re-elected as described.

Section F: Removal of Officers
Leadership may be revoked without a mutual agreement for non-participation, misconduct, failure to fulfill job duties, or violations of any provisions of the Constitution. The officer will be notified in writing of the possible removal from office at least 72 hours prior to the vote and will be allowed to address the organization to relate to members any relevant defense prior to the voting for removal. Any officer may be removed from office upon a 2/3 affirmative vote of active student members. The removed officer shall provide all documents relating to the organization and brief their replacement of current projects in their care.

Section G: Resignation
Officers no longer wishing to serve on the board must submit their resignation to the President (or Vice President if the President is resigning) and advisor at least two (2) weeks in advance. Prior to the officer's final day, they shall provide all documents relating to the organization and brief their replacement of current projects in their care.

Section H: Filling Vacant Officer Positions
In the event an officer (besides President) is removed or resigns, the remaining officers will decide if the position is to be filled. If it is to be filled, the nomination and election process will occur at the next membership meeting. The officers may appoint an interim officer to serve in the vacant position until the next membership meeting.

If the President is removed or resigns, the Vice President will assume the role of President upon a majority confirmation of the remaining officers. If not confirmed, the position of the President will be filled as per the paragraph above.

The newly elected officer's term shall end at the annual installation of officers in April. A change in officer information should be reported to the University within ten school days of the election.

ARTICLE VIII STUDENT ORGANIZATION ADVISOR

The student organization advisor shall serve as a resource person and provide advisory support for the organization's officers and members. If the student organization advisor is unable to continue in their position, officers may nominate a replacement at any time, to be confirmed by a majority vote of the members.

ARTICLE IX FINANCES

There are no membership dues.

ARTICLE X DISSOLUTION OF ORGANIZATION

In the event this organization dissolves, all monies left in the treasury, after outstanding debts and claims have been paid, shall be donated to a charity of choice.

ARTICLE XI AMENDMENTS

Amendments to the constitution must be proposed in writing to the President. The amendment must then be presented to the organization during a membership meeting and include a full explanation and/or rationale for the amendment. The amendment must be voted on at the following membership meeting and approved by a 2/3 affirmative vote of active student members. All amended constitutions must be submitted to the University within two school weeks. The amendment shall not take effect until approved by Boston University.

FOUNDATION STUDIES— ADDITIONAL FOLLOW-UP BIBLE STUDIES

THE FIRST FIVE follow-up Bible studies in our fellowship's First Principles series need to be done quickly with the new student baptisms. Even after these, though, it is crucial to continue building their spiritual foundation with a continued one-on-one Bible study on different Christian convictions. *Foundations* is a study series with additional follow-up Bible studies I developed to help new converts build a strong foundation.

1. Prayer, Power, and the Holy Spirit
2. Bible Study: Hearing the Voice of God
3. Faith and Obedience
4. The Grace of God
5. Discipling Partners

6. Prepared for Church
7. Heaven, Hell, and the Final Judgment
8. Relationships in the Body
9. The Sermon on the Mount
10. Discipline

PRAYER, POWER, & THE HOLY SPIRIT

Introduction:
Discuss how essential communication is in building any relationship, especially in your relationship with God! Prayer is speaking to God and the key to having a powerful relationship with Him.

Plan and Prioritize Prayer

Mark 1:35
Jesus was a busy man but made time to pray
He found a place and time free from distractions
He prayed early in the morning **(Psalm 5:3)**

Matthew 6:5-8
Prayer is personal with God and not for show
Discuss a Good place to have your prayer spot
Pray with purpose and pour out your heart

Luke 11:1-13
Prayer is learned and not natural
Pray with other Christians to learn to pray

Prevented Prayers (Hindrances to prayer life and reasons for unanswered prayer)

1 Peter 4:7—lack of clear-mindedness or focus
Psalm 66:18—unrepentant or unconfessed sin
Proverbs 28:9—not Reading your Bible
Proverbs 21:13—ignoring the cry of the poor
Luke 18:1-8—no persistence or giving up praying

Mark 11:24—lack of faith

1 John 5:14—it is not in God's Will

Power—The Holy Spirit

Acts 2:38; 5:32

The Holy Spirit is received at baptism

The Holy Spirit is given from God as a gift that gives you the
power to live the Christian life

Ephesians 5:17-20; Colossians 3:16

Being *"filled with the Spirit"* means to be spiritual or godly
(i.e., glass filled up, no room for anything else)

Singing songs to God and one another, reading the Bible,
and discipling each other are how Christians continually
fill themselves with God's Spirit

Ezekiel 36:26-27; John 16:5-13

The Holy Spirit will always lead you to the Word of God, *"all
truth."* Emotions or your feelings are not the Holy Spirit if
it conflicts with God's Word **(Psalm 143:10)**

The Holy Spirit tells us what the Father says through the
Bible since He is one with God, is God, and was God's
agent to author the Scriptures **(2 Peter 1:20-21)**

Ephesians 6:18; Jude 20

Praying *"in the Spirit"* is simply being spiritual when you
pray and praying according to God's Word, as discussed
above—also, praying through passages in the Bible

Praying for other Christians is praying in the Spirit

Acts 8:29-30; 2 Timothy 1:7

The Spirit helps you in your evangelism

The Spirit is one of discipline and order

Discuss whom you have felt led to share with this week

Practical

Write out a prayer list

Decide a place and time to pray every day that is free from distractions

BIBLE STUDY: HEARING THE VOICE OF GOD

Introduction

Discuss the previous study's main topic: how we communicate with God. Today's Bible study is how we listen to God.

Foundation

Luke 6:46-49

It is not enough to just hear the word; we must put it into practice.

Digging deep into the Bible will build your foundation on the rock to weather the storms of life.

Discuss with one another various times when the Bible helped you weather the trials of life.

Psalm 1:2-3

Delight in the word of God. It is essential to enjoy Bible study.

Digging deep comes by meditating on the Bible. Memorize verses.

The Bible helps us to prosper in everyday life.

Temptation

Matthew 4:1-11

Just as we eat daily for nutrition, the Bible needs to be "digested" daily for spiritual growth. Physically we depend on food to survive, so we must study the Bible to survive spiritually.

Jesus fought temptation from the devil by quoting the Bible. He hid the word of God in His heart and therefore had it on His mind.

Satan knows the Bible well and will use it against us by teaching it falsely. The enemy's twisting of Scripture is why there is so much false doctrine, and it is important we are in the Bible daily so we aren't deceived.

Psalm 119:9-11

Living according to the Bible will keep us pure.

Hiding the word in our hearts prevents us from sinning against God.

Choose a day to read **Psalm 119** in its entirety to fall in love with the Bible.

Education

Acts 17:10-12

Eagerly examine the Scriptures every day.

Make decisions based on what you read.

1 Peter 3:15; 2 Timothy 2:15

Studying the Bible will equip us to handle the Bible correctly in studying with others.

It will also equip us to be prepared to answer people's questions.

Become a student of God's word.

Practicals

Read the New Testament first, and then go back and read through the whole Bible.

Ask the person discipling you what would be a good reading plan.

Plan a time every morning to pray and read your Bible.

SHARE: SPECKS Acronym—what to look for when reading.

Sin to be avoided

Prayers or **P**raise to be given

Examples to follow or not follow

Commands to be obeyed

Knowledge to learn

Share with someone

Pray to God before, during, and after your time in God's Word for Him to open your mind to understand the Scriptures. (Luke 24:45)

FAITH & OBEDIENCE

Hebrews 11:1, 6

> Faith is a certainty in things not seen and the hope we have in God.
>
> Without faith, it is impossible to please God.
>
> God rewards those who earnestly seek Him.

James 2:14-20

> We are responsible for meeting needs in the body of Christ.
>
> Faith without action is dead.
>
> The demons believe but will not be in heaven as it takes obedience as well.

1 Samuel 15:1-26

> Saul was sent on a mission from God but did not obey. **(vs. 1-9)**
>
> God is grieved when we do not obey. **(vs. 10-11)**
>
> Saul thought he had obeyed, made a monument in his honor, and made excuses. All follow our choices that lead to our being self-deceived. **(vs. 12-21)**
>
> Saul's lack of obedience led God to reject him. **(vs. 22-26)**

1 Kings 13:1-26 (The Man of God from Judah.)

> God gives us specific instructions that must be obeyed.
>
> The main challenge is not to be deceived into trusting man's word over God's perfect Word.
>
> Defiance of God's Word spells spiritual death. Trust God's Word over religious teachings.

2 Kings 5:1-14

Naaman had a physical need to be cured of his leprosy. **(vv. 1-7)**

Naaman did not like the advice Elisha told him. **(vv. 8-12)**

Naaman listened to the servants, went, and obeyed—then he was cured. **(vv. 13-14)**

John 14:15

We show our love for God by obeying Him.

Through obedience, we love God the way He wants to be loved

1 John 2:3-6

Obedience shows how much we know God.

God's love is perfected in obedience.

Ephesians 2:8-10

We are saved by grace through faith (obedience).

Hebrews 11:30—Walls of Jericho—faith (believe the walls will come down by God), and obedience—(march around seven days, seven times). Who brought down the walls? God.

SHARE: Captain analogy—if you are drowning and the captain throws a lifesaver out to save you, what must you do? Grab it! Who saved you? The captain, the lifesaver, or yourself? ALL three! Captain = God; Lifesaver = Jesus; you grabbing it = conditions God sets/obedience.

Acts 26:19

I was not disobedient to the vision from heaven.

God has a vision for you that will be lived out through faith and obedience.

THE GRACE OF GOD

Definition: Grace is a gift, blessing, or favor brought to man by God at Christ's death on the cross.

Analogy: Golden Gate Bridge/Safety Net

Ephesians 2:8-10—Grace saved us

We are saved by grace. Salvation is a gift from God.

God saved us from our sins. Recall your baptism and the joy of being saved.

Faith was the condition to receive God's gift of grace. (**Col. 2:12**)

Analogy: 3 Options—revenge, law, forgiveness—which one is grace? None.

Titus 2:11-14—Grace teaches us to say no to ungodliness

Discuss how grace could teach us to say no to sin.

Biblical grace always produces godliness and self-control.

Grace can be abused. (**Jude 1:4; Romans 6:1-2**)

Jesus gave Himself to redeem us from sin and produce an eagerness to do good works.

1 Corinthians 15:9-11—Grace motivates us to work hard for God

Grace motivated Paul to work hard.

Discuss the apostle Paul's life. How did grace practically impact Paul? (1 Tim. 1:12-16)

Knowing who we are without God and what we deserve helps us appreciate God's grace even more.

To the extent we understand grace is proportionate to how hard we will work for God.

Luke 19:10-27—Grace helps us to be evangelistic

Minas represent our salvation, the servants are us as disciples, and the king is Jesus.

We are not saved by works but saved to work. God expects us to invest our salvation into others by sharing our faith. (**Luke 19:10-11**)

The third servant cheapened the grace of God by burying it and thus keeping it to himself.

2 Corinthians 5:14—Christ's love compels us to share our faith.

Discuss how it has been going with personal evangelism.

Romans 5:1-2—Stand in grace

You have been justified. (**Analogy:** Justified = "Just as if I'd" never sinned)

God has given us access and fellowship to himself through grace.

Prayer is key to understanding grace deeper. (**Eph. 3:14-19**)

Confession helps us keep our confidence in God's grace. (**1 John 1:5-10**)

Practical

Confess any known sin and embrace God's grace today. Decide to pray to understand grace deeper and be motivated to work hard for God.

DISCIPLING PARTNERS

Introduction

In the church, everyone has someone assigned to be their "discipler." Discipling is God's plan to evangelize the nations. By nature, God is a relational being (i.e., the Trinity). There are 59 "one-another" verses in the Bible and many great examples of discipling relationships: Moses-Joshua, Samuel-Saul, Samuel-David, Elijah-Elisha, Nathan-David, Jesus-the twelve, Barnabas-Paul, Paul-Timothy, Peter-Mark, etc. Discipling requires qualities that please God, such as submission, humility, faith, trust, and love.

Matthew 28:18-20—Discipling is a command of God

Every new baptized Christian is to have a teacher/discipler.

It begins even before baptism.

There is a difference between teaching someone to obey and teaching the Bible.

Analogy: Changing a Tire—Do not use the manual; you are taught to obey.

We need a flesh and blood example to follow. (**John 1:14, 1 Corinthians 11:1**)

Exodus 18:13-27—The structure of discipling in the church

The "Jethro Principle" is how we set up discipling relationships so every disciple's spiritual needs can be met.

Discuss the purpose of House Churches, Bible Talks, and Discipling Partners.

Four generations of discipling: Paul → Timothy → Reliable Men → Others. (**2 Tim. 2:1-2**)

We should have a submissive spirit in our relationships and the structure the church leadership has decided. (**Eph. 5:21, Heb. 13:7, 17**)

Colossians 1:28-29—The goal of discipling relationships

To present each other mature in Christ is the goal of discipleship.

Discipling takes labor and energy, which God supplies.

The Bible holds the authority in discipling.

We need to be trained by others. Discipling is based on friendship, trust, and love. (**Luke 6:39-40**)

Imitate the Christ-like attributes of your discipler. (**1 Cor. 4:14-17**)

Discipleship is more than just a time to confess and pray, but also it is a time to train to become more like Jesus and better at making other disciples.

Attitude in discipling

James 5:16-17—need to confess sins to another person. Transparency is essential.

Proverbs 10:17; 15:12—love discipline and correction.

Proverbs 11:14; 12:15—initiate discipling. Ask a lot of advice across all domains of life: ministry, finances, moving, dating, missing services, career, etc.

Hebrews 3:12-13—Discipleship is daily

There should be daily communication with your discipler. This prevents the heart from hardening.

Sin is deceitful by nature, so we need someone else who can see our blind spots spiritually.

Practically: Have a once-a-week "discipleship time" (D-time) with your discipler. Have a plan to communicate daily.

John 15:1-17—Discipleship is staying connected

Jesus was the perfect disciple of God. He shared what He had received with those He discipled.

Discipling is how someone remains in the vine.

Discipling requires obedience, love, and sacrifice.

The goal is to produce much fruit.

PREPARED FOR CHURCH

Introduction
Hebrews 12:28-29—Congregational worship is one of the most powerful times of Christian growth. We need to make sure we worship God in an acceptable way which requires preparation.

Connection

Quiet Time (**Heb. 10:19-25**)
Draw near to God prior to coming to service. Be spiritually prepared to give of yourself to others. Church is not about us but God and the spiritual family.
Consider how you may spur your brothers and sisters on toward love and good deeds.
Do not miss the worship assemblies.

Plan for Visitors (**Acts 9:10-11**)
Jesus told Ananias specifically how to preach the gospel to Paul.
You should give the address of service or have planned a ride for your visitors—the earlier in the week the better!
Think through which disciples would relate well and be encouraging for your visitors to fellowship.

Singing and Praise (**Eph. 5:18-20**)
Singing to God and one another fills us with the Holy Spirit.
We are commanded to sing from our hearts. Discuss using a songbook or paying attention to the projection of the words.

Fellowship with other disciples at church by asking about what God is teaching them about worship. Strive to have deep relationships.

Zeal (**Rom. 12:11; Neh. 8:4-6**) Shout amen (means "so be it") or clap your hands when something hits you from the lesson. Do not be afraid to engage and be vocal during service! This zealous feedback encourages God and the speakers to give their whole hearts.

Communion

Purpose of Communion (**1 Cor. 11:23-32**)
Jesus initiated it at Passover before His death. (**Mark 14:22-26**)
To remember and proclaim Jesus' death. (**1 Cor. 11:26**)
Communion was taken on Sunday in the early church. (**Acts 20:7**)
To stay strong spiritually. (**1 Cor. 11:30**)

Preparing for Communion (**1 Cor. 11:28**)
Confess any known sin before service. (**1 John 1:5-10, James 5:16-17**)
Reconcile any relationships before service. (**Matt. 5:23-24**)
Note: you initiate the reconciliation even if you remember someone has something towards you.
The consequences of not taking communion properly include becoming spiritually weak, getting sick, or even falling away eventually. God wants us always to remember the Cross.

Contribution

How We Collect Weekly Contribution

We imitate Paul's pattern for his collection to the poor
Christians in Jerusalem and give our contribution every
Sunday. (**1 Cor. 16:1-2**)

Paul practiced accountability here.

We use envelopes/weekly pledge for accountability.

Leadership has decided to use the Old Testament principle
of tithing as a guideline in our congregation. Tithing is
not the ceiling but the foundation (a good starting point).
Jesus encouraged sacrifice. (**Luke 14:33; Heb. 13:17**)

Every member pledges an amount to give weekly. Must
stick to our commitment even when going out of town.
(**Eccles. 5:4**)

Why We Collect Weekly Contribution

We are giving first to God (**Mal. 3:6-12; 2 Cor. 9:6-8**).

We support our ministry leaders and staff. (**1 Cor. 9:14;
Phil. 4:14-19; Titus 3:13-14**)

If we are giving to God, we will trust him and the leaders
who decide how the money is used. If leadership ever sins
in using the money, God will still bless the pure heart that
gave to Him. The widow was commended by Jesus for
her giving, even though it was given to a corrupt religious
institution (**Luke 21:1-4**).

Discuss how our churches are transparent about their
finances and hold annual financial presentations for the
church members.

Prepared to Give

Come to service having gone to the ATM or written your check or having already given the night before via PayPal. **(Deut. 16:16b—principle)**

Walk in the light concerning your financial situation. Be open right away if you feel you will not be able to give to God that week.

God will bless your sacrifice.

HEAVEN, HELL, AND THE FINAL JUDGEMENT

Introduction

Discuss your thoughts on what eternity will be like.

Revelation 20:11-15

The one thing all men have in common is we will all stand before God and be judged.

How we live life here on earth will determine our eternal fate.

There will be a day we will all be resurrected to be judged by God. (**John 5:28-30**)

Two books, one is a record of how we lived and the other is the book of life.

Those whose names are not in the book of life will spend an eternity in Hell.

Matthew 25:31-46

At the final judgment, God will take into account how we lived our lives and if we knew Jesus.

Hell was not originally prepared for humans, but for the Devil and his angels. (**v.41**)

The punishment in Hell is eternal. (**v.46**) Jesus talked about Hell more than He did Heaven.

Matthew 7:13-14, 21-23

Hell is the default place people are headed since they all sin. (**Rom. 3:23**) The road to Heaven is narrow.

Many religious people will be in Hell since they did not follow God's word.

People choose to go to Hell by rejecting God for their sin.

Jesus must know us as his disciples/children to be saved.

Revelation 21:8; Hebrews 10:26-31

Those that persist in their sin will be in Hell.

Discuss the list of sins that describe those who go to Hell.

Deliberate and willful sin as a disciple can cause us to forfeit our salvation and go to Hell.

No self-righteous person will be in Heaven. We must believe we deserve to go to Hell, but by God's grace, He gives us eternal life if we are a disciple. (**Luke 18:14, Rom. 6:23**)

Luke 16:19-31

Hell is irreversible once there. Our choices in life have eternal consequences.

Once we have died, our fate is sealed for eternity. There is no purgatory or second chance. (**v.26**)

Hell includes eternal torment, fire, regret, thirst, despair, and agony.

This man became very evangelistic in Hell, but it was too late. Hell should motivate us to share our faith with our friends and family now before their time is gone (**2 Cor. 5:11**). Fear God.

Luke 12:2-7

Having a fear of God and Hell is healthy and Jesus encouraged it. (**Ex. 20:20**)

God cares deeply about us and desires no man to go to Hell but all to be saved. He talks about Hell out of His love for us—to warn us so we won't choose to go there. (**1 Tim. 2:3-4**)

John 14:1-4

Jesus is preparing a room for us in Heaven, so we should not let our hearts be troubled.

God understands that we will be motivated by being rewarded at times.

Matthew 6:19-21

We will be rewarded treasures in Heaven.

How we live here on earth and what our heart is centered on will determine the rewards we receive in Heaven.

Revelation 21:1-4

We will be in God's presence in Heaven, and a whole new life of eternity awaits us.

There will be no more tears, death, pain, or old ways in Heaven.

Practicals

Confess and repent of any sin that is on your heart after this study.

Read Revelation 21-22, which is a symbolic picture of Heaven. Write down what you think Heaven may be like and get excited knowing we are citizens of Heaven. (**Phil. 3:20-21**)

RELATIONSHIPS IN THE KINGDOM

Introduction
How close are you to the brothers and sisters in the church? Discuss.

The importance of relationships in the kingdom (Mark 3:31-35)
Doing God's will makes us Jesus' brother or sister with God as our father.

The church family must come before even our physical family.

It will only be the church family that helps us do God's will and get to Heaven.

The purpose of relationships in the kingdom (John 13:34-35)
Jesus commands us to love the disciples.

Our love for one for another makes us distinct as Christians.

We cannot be isolated Christians. Disciples need fellowship.

Discuss if anyone is hard to love and decide to follow Jesus' command to love.

The need for relationships in the kingdom (Heb. 3:12-14)
Daily encouragement protects our hearts from getting hard and from sin.

Discuss why it is important to go on dates in the kingdom to encourage our brothers/sisters.

Decide ways you can encourage other brothers and sisters this week.

Kingdom relationships:
Build one another up with words (**Eph. 4:29**).

Submit to one another in humility. (**Phil. 2:3-4; Eph. 5:21**)

They are focused on each other's spiritual growth. (**Col. 1:28**)
Have a sincere love that is from the heart. (**1 Pet. 1:22**)
Sacrifice for one another since Jesus is our example. (**1 John 3:16**)

When problems arise in kingdom relationships (Matt. 18:15-17)

Discuss the steps Jesus commands us to take if we are sinned against in the church. (**Gal. 6:1-2**)
We cannot allow bitterness to grow in our hearts towards our brothers or sisters. (**Heb. 12:14-15**)
It is our responsibility to make every effort to be at peace with everyone. (**SHARE:** Poison)

Relationship with God produces amazing kingdom relationships (1 John 2:9-10)

If our relationships in the body are not good, our relationship with God is not right.
This correlation implies that a strong relationship with God will produce strong relationships in the church.

Dating Relationships in the kingdom (2 Cor. 6:14-18)

Disciples date and marry only disciples. (**SHARE:** Yoke— held animals together)
We must treat the opposite sex as our siblings with absolute purity. (**1 Tim. 5:1-2**)
Single Christians should consistently go on "encouragement dates" to protect our brothers' and sisters' hearts from temptation in the world. (**Heb. 3:12-13**)
In the church, we go on "double dates" to maintain purity and build great friendships. (**Ephesians 5:3-7**)

Practicals (Acts 2:42-47)

Make a plan this next week to encourage a disciple every day.

Plan a double-date with brothers and sisters you do not know very well if you are single. If married, go out with a couple in the church you do not know very well.

Discuss how much you are invested into the kingdom at a relational level and take it higher.

THE SERMON ON THE MOUNT

Introduction

Matthew was written to a Jewish audience, and Jesus being on the mount giving a sermon would have reminded them of Moses bringing the Law down from Mount Sinai in the Old Testament. One greater than Moses, Jesus, would bring "new laws" for how men and women would live in his kingdom, the church. Read through this sermon together and discuss points that strike you in your walk with God.

TEXT: Matthew 5-7—LIFE IN THE KINGDOM

Kingdom Attitudes (Matt. 5:1-12)

Go through and discuss what each of the beatitudes means. Jesus isn't just concerned with just our behavior but our attitude as well.

"Blessed" means happy! How are these attitudes different from what the world teaches us?

Persecution is promised to anyone who takes a stand for Jesus.

Kingdom Evangelism (Matt. 5:13-16)

Salt is a preservative. We must keep our saltiness.

Disciples are the light of the world—not just the community. World evangelism must be in the heart.

Our deeds must be on display for people to see a difference. Discuss how you are doing being a light at your job, school, and family.

Kingdom Righteousness (Matt. 5:17-20)

Discuss the role of the Old Testament in the kingdom.

Jesus Christ fulfilled the Mosaic Law.

To enter the kingdom, our righteousness must surpass that of the Pharisees.

The Pharisees knew the Scriptures and practiced many religiously devout deeds. How could our righteousness surpass such rigorous devotion? Jesus is concerned about the heart.

Kingdom Laws

Law against hate and anger. Hate/anger = murder in God's eyes. Must settle matters quickly. (**Matt. 5:21-26**)

Law against adultery and lust. Lust = adultery in God's eyes. Hell is a reality if one does not repent. Must deal radically with sin by cutting it out of your life. (**Matt. 5:27-30**)

Law against divorce. Marriage is sacred and final in God's eyes. The only exception for divorce is adultery and abandonment. (See **1 Cor. 7**; **Matt. 5:31-32**)

Law for integrity. In the kingdom, your word is your word. (**Matt. 5:33-37**)

Law against retaliation. (**Matt. 5:38-41**)

Law of love towards enemies. We are to be like our heavenly Father. (**Matt. 5:43-48**)

Kingdom Disciplines

Jesus emphasizes our hearts not to do spiritual disciplines for show or to be noticed, but rather to do them because we want to be close to God.

Giving to the needy. Explain benevolence on Wednesday evenings. This should also be a normal part of our lives as disciples. This is different from our weekly contribution. (**Matt. 6:1-4**)

Praying to God. Have a place of prayer and eliminate distractions. Review the model of prayer Jesus gives. (**Matt. 6:5-15**)

Fasting. Jesus says, *"when you fast..."* This assumes that fasting is a normal part of the Christian life in the kingdom. (**Matt. 6:16-18**)

Storing up Treasure

Have a healthy/generous eye. Giving purifies our whole spirit. You cannot be greedy and serve God. Our spiritual disciplines store up for us treasure in heaven. (**Matt. 6:19-24**)

Do not allow the treasures of this earth to cause you anxiety. When we worry, we lack faith. Seek first the kingdom (community of God/Church) and his righteousness (personal relationship with Christ), and all will be provided for you. (**Matt. 6:25-34**)

Kingdom Convictions

No Hypocrisy (Matt. 7:1-6)

Jesus is not teaching that we never make judgments. (See **1 Cor. 5:12**)

Some have misused this passage as an excuse to tolerate sin in the lives of others.

Jesus is teaching that we must not be hypocritical. We cannot preach to others if we are living in the same sins.

If you share the gospel with someone who is not open to it or continues to live in hypocrisy (dogs/pigs), it can end up coming back to hurt us.

The Golden Rule (Matt. 7:7-12)

God promises that anyone who keeps asking, seeking, and knocking will find Him.

God blesses us even though we are evil.

We need to treat others the way we would want to be treated.

This sums up the Old Testament according to Jesus.

The Narrow Road (Matt. 7:13-27)

Few are truly saved. Discuss why this is. Review the plan of salvation. (**Acts 2:36-42**)

Even in Noah's day, only eight people in the entire world were saved. (**1 Pet. 3:16-22**)

False prophets are the reason people miss the narrow road. We will recognize them by the fruit of their teaching.

Just because someone says Jesus is Lord does not mean they are saved.

They must not only hear the word of God but practice it to build their foundation strong.

Conclusion (Matt. 7:28-29)

Jesus spoke with authority. We can speak with authority when preaching the Word of God.

There is a difference between being religious and having deep convictions.

DISCIPLINE

Introduction

The word "disciple" and "discipline" come from the same root word. Jesus is the perfect example of a disciplined life. God gave us His Spirit, which manifests as a spirit of self-discipline (**2 Tim. 1:7**). If we live disciplined lives, we are living in the power of the Spirit.

Disciplined with our Quiet Times (Josh. 1:8; Mark 1:35-39)

To meditate on the Word day and night implies the discipline of memorization.

Jesus was up while it was still dark. He took time to get spiritually ready for the day.

Getting up early requires the discipline of getting enough sleep. Do not hit the snooze button on your alarm. You need undistracted time to spend with God and power up for the day. Jesus was ready to take on the task of evangelizing after His time with God.

Practicals

Have a book of the Bible you are studying out.

Start by praying for an hour every day. Time it if you need to discipline your mind and body.

Get advice on how to have great Quiet Times.

Disciplined with our Schedule (Jer. 29:11-14; Luke 13:32)

God has a plan for your life. We are to imitate God. (**Eph. 5:1**) This means we should have a plan.

Jesus did not live aimlessly but lived according to the mission God gave Him.

Every disciple should have a planner. You prioritize your week with the kingdom first. (**Matt. 6:33**)

Practicals

    Use Sunday or Monday to take time and plan out your week. Plan quiet times, meetings of the body, Bible studies, discipleship times, dates, gym time, etc.

    Obey your schedule. If you are not used to living a disciplined life, let your discipleship partner know your schedule for accountability.

    Plan to have one day to use the morning time to rest. The principle of the Sabbath.

Disciplined with our Purity (Matt. 5:27-30; 1 Thess. 4:3-8)

Jesus teaches we must be radical to be pure.

God's will is that we discipline our bodies and minds for purity by living self-controlled lives.

Impurity is a rejection of discipline and the Holy Spirit. The pure in heart will see God. (**Matt. 5:8**)

Married disciples should have an active sex life to prevent temptation from Satan. (**1 Cor. 7:5**)

Practicals

    Avoid situations that tempt you to be impure (put accountability software on your devices, avoid people, places, and situations that are tempting, etc.)

    If married, plan times of intimacy in your schedule with your spouse.

    If single, be very open about sin and temptation. Satan's goal is to keep you in the darkness about this area. (**1 John 1:5-10**)

Disciplined with our Money (Mark 12:41-44; Prov. 13:11)

> Jesus commends those who are sacrificial in their giving to God.
>
> It is not about how much money you have, but how you are giving to God first and from your heart.
>
> There are no shortcuts to financial discipline. Jesus expects us to be stewards of our money so we can use our wealth to win souls in the kingdom. (**Luke 16:1-13**)
>
> Practicals
>
>> Can you give more in your weekly contribution than you are currently giving?
>>
>> Avoid pyramid schemes or get rich quick schemes.
>>
>> Financial transparency is key to growing spiritually. Set up a time to go over your budget with one of the financially astute shepherds in the church.

Disciplined with our Health (1 Cor. 6:19-20; 10:31; 3 John 2; 1 Tim. 4:8)

> Our bodies house the Holy Spirit and must be taken care of. Mental health is also part of our temple (brain). Is there medicine you have been prescribed you should be taking?
>
> We need to consider when we eat and drink—does it glorify God?
>
> The apostle John hoped his church was in good health.
>
> Physical training is of some value, according to Paul.
>
> Practicals
>
>> Take up a sport, join a health club or gym, take a walk before going to bed, etc.
>>
>> Invite accountability in this area of your life. Join a program (i.e., weight watchers, etc.).

Get regular check-ups from your doctor.

Talk to your discipler about a weekly plan to stay healthy. Maybe visit a nutritionist. Everyone's body is different so take time to research to find out what will help you.

Conclusion: What areas from this study do you need empowerment by the Holy Spirit to transform your life? Make radical decisions and watch the Holy Spirit empower you to do even greater things for God.

FIVE BIBLE TALK OUTLINES YOU CAN DO ON CAMPUS

THE VALIDITY OF THE BIBLE

OPENING: Share your name and have the first person who shares whisper something into the next person's ear. Every person that shares must whisper what was said. Have the last person who says their name say out loud what was whispered (*Telephone game*).

Q: How come with so few people, it is still challenging to find out what was originally whispered? (Perception, volume, language barriers, etc.)

Q: What could have helped us make sure what was whispered was not changed as it traveled from one person to another? (Write it down and pass a paper around.)

Q: What are some common myths you have heard about the Bible?

Today we are going to look at Peter's understanding of Scripture. Peter was one of the closest Apostles to Jesus Christ. He writes **2 Peter** some 37 years after he had walked with Jesus Christ. **2 Peter** was written in 64 A.D. shortly before the Roman Emperor Nero killed Peter in 68 A.D.

2 Peter 1:16-18

Q: How is Peter defending the faith in this verse? (Claims he was there, heard God's voice—**Matt. 17**)

Q: Is eyewitness testimony reliable? Why or why not?

Q: In what ways does our society value eyewitness testimony? (Justice system)

Q: Is there a double standard when it comes to the Bible? Why would this be?

Q: What does it take to make up a cleverly devised story?

Q: Could the Apostles and early followers of Jesus do this? Why or why not? (ref. **1 Cor. 15:6**—over 500 witnesses to the resurrection, most the Apostles died a martyr's death.)

Q: Would you die for a lie? (Discuss historical evidence of Jesus, etc.)

Q: How many of you would love to hear the audible voice of God? (Peter claims they heard the voice of God on the Mountain of Transfiguration.) **What would be your "ideal" way for God to prove Himself to you?**

This audible voice is still based solely on eyewitness testimony and a game of "telephone" in a sense, but at least it is written down. Let us see if there is something more reliable for us.

2 Peter 2:19-21

Q: What did Peter see as completely reliable (some translations made "more certain")? (Peter saw the Scripture as more reliable than the voice of God from heaven! And the prophecies were all fulfilled or *"made more certain"* (NIV 1984)—by Jesus' life!

Q: How would the Bible be more reliable than a voice from heaven?

Q: Peter says, "Above all"—what does he, above all, want us to understand? (That Scripture was authored by God using men as vessels.)

Q: Is there such a thing as interpretation according to the Bible? (No private interpretation)

Q: How do we get rid of interpretation? Do we all not interpret? (It is not about getting rid of interpretation but learning to interpret the right way. God had a specific message, and it would not mean something different today than it meant to the original hearers).

FACTS:

- Bible is 66 books
- Written by 40 different authors (some kings, tax collectors, poor people, etc.)
- Written on 3 different continents
- Written in 3 different languages (Hebrew, Greek, some Aramaic)
- All in 1500-2000 years

Amazing, as there are no contradictions, and the Bible tells one story about one God. If we all witnessed a crime, chances are when we write the police report, there may be discrepancies, and yet in the Bible, with many authors who were not contemporaries, we do not find those discrepancies!

2 Peter 2:1-2

Q: Why do false teachers introduce destructive heresies?

Q: What is the consequence of following false teaching?

2 Peter 3:14-18

Q: What is Peter most concerned about in some of his last words before he would be crucified upside down by Nero? (Make sure to not fall into error or false teaching!)

Q: Can the Bible be hard to understand? (Yes, even in this time, people were distorting Paul's letters to say what they wanted it to say—this leads to their destruction spiritually)

Q: What would it look like to make every effort to be found at peace with God (v.14)?

It has been an amazing Bible discussion today. Consider, do you know the Scriptures?

CHALLENGE: Study the Bible with the person who brought you to make sure you understand God's will for your life.

The Final Exam

> **OPENING:** What is your name, and how do you imagine the final judgment?

Q: As we get ready for our exams or finals week, what type of feelings do we have? (Fear, anxiety, stress, etc.)

Q: Why do we have these types of feelings? (Exams determine whether we will graduate!)

Q: When do you ever feel great about a test? (When you know the information or the test is going to be easy.)

Many people will sacrifice long hours, tuition money, and energy to take classes and exams to get a degree, but are you ready for the ultimate final exam...judgment day?

Revelation 20:11-15—There are two things everyone in this room has in common, everyone will die at some point, and secondly, everyone will face God for judgment.

Q: Do most people think about judgment day? Why or why not?

Q: What is opened before God in this passage? (Many books)

I want to talk today about three books:

1. The Book of Life
Q: If your name is not written in the Book of Life, what are the consequences? (Lake of fire/hell)

Q: From this verse, what determines whether your name is written in the book of life or not? (deeds)

Interesting, it does not say faith, grace, or how much you prayed but by your deeds!

2. The Book of Deeds
If the Book of Life shows who is saved, what do the other books contain? (Your life's deeds)

Imagine a TV in this room that began to play good and bad deeds in front of this whole group.

Q: How would you feel?

The Bible teaches that Jesus will judge us based on how we lived.

Q: Do you think it is fair that Jesus judges us based on our deeds? (discuss)

Q: What does "Christendom" today teach that determines whether we make it to heaven or not? (Nothing, since they teach we are not saved by works.)

Ephesians 2:8-10

Wait…if works do not save us, how come we are judged by our deeds/works? (Have a fun discussion)

All Scripture has context…read on **v.11-13**

Q: So what works is this verse referring to? (Works of the Old Testament law, i.e., circumcision, etc.)

Now we know for a fact that the deeds Jesus will judge us on are not Old Testament Mosaic Law deeds such as sacrificing animals or whether you are circumcised or not.

Q: So, what deeds are they? (Commands in the New Testament, Jesus' teachings, etc.)

Q: Through what does the Bible say we are saved? (Faith)

James 2:14-19, 24

Q: What do deeds reflect? (Faith!)

Q: Are demons saved? Why not? (No. They believe but do not have deeds—thus no true faith.)

Q: Why do so many "Christians" today teach we are saved by faith alone and that deeds do not count for anything? (Easier path, misunderstanding of what grace is, demons influence others to have their type of "faith," etc.)

Will you have a demonic faith (faith only) or a biblical faith (faith shown by deeds)?

3. *The Bible*

Q: We know deeds are now necessary for saving faith, but how would we know what deeds Jesus is looking for? (The Bible)

You see, we may not have the Book of Life or the Book of Deeds here on earth since God has those in heaven, but we do have The Book... The Bible is the standard that is going to be used in our judgment.

John 12:48- Jesus will use His word to judge us.

Imagine your professor will give you a pass/fail exam, and it depends on whether you study the textbook. The Bible is our textbook for The Final Exam/Judgment, yet unlike a textbook, it must be studied and lived out.

Q: What are some ways students get ready for a final exam? (Study, get tutoring, have a professor, study groups, discipline, consistent repetition, etc.)

Q: Using those same principles, what would it look like to study to get ready for Judgment Day? (Study the Bible, get someone who knows the Bible to teach it to you, be disciplined in studying and reading it, etc.)

CHALLENGE: Study the Bible today with the person who brought you to pass The Final!

WHAT IS TRUTH?

OPENING: Pass around your Bible and have everyone introduce themselves while guessing how many inches in length the Bible is.

Q: How come everyone gave different measurements? (Everyone has different perspectives.)

Q: How would we find out the right measurement? (Use a ruler)

Pull out the ruler and measure it. Give candy or a reward to the person who was the closest.

John 18:37-38

Q: What does everyone on the side of truth do? (Listen to Jesus)

Q: What are different ideas of truth today? (Science, religion, experience, feelings, etc.)

Q: Is there an absolute truth in this world? (If they say there is no absolute truth, that statement itself is an absolute truth. Share how life shows us there are absolutes—math, for example, 1 + 1 always = 2.)

Q: What do people base truth on? (Family, tradition, religion, etc.).

Let us listen to Jesus as He taught about how to find the truth.

John 8:31-32

Q: Did the Jews believe? (Yes)

Q: Just because they believed, did that mean they knew the truth? (No)

Q: How does one find out the truth? (They must hold to the teachings of Jesus.)

Q: Where do we find Jesus' teachings? (The Bible)

John 17:17

Q: What is the truth here? (Jesus is the Word.)

Q: What are some current "trending" opinions about the Bible?

Q: Are the world's current views of truth we discussed earlier working or making things worse?

The Bible is the truth and can transform lives for eternity. It is composed of 66 books, written by 40 different authors, on three different continents, over 1500 years, and yet it tells one story with no contradictions!

Q: How did we find out the truth of this Bible's length at the beginning of the Bible Talk? (Measured it with a ruler.)

Q: How do we find out if we are right with God? (Measure ourselves with the 'ruler'—the Word of God!)

> **CHALLENGE:** Listen to Jesus, be on the side of truth, and study the Bible to see how your life measures up to God's standard.

HOT/COLD, OR LUKEWARM?

OPENING: Have everyone go around and say their name and how their relationship with God is going.

Revelation 3:14-22 (Begin by discussing the passage with the following questions.)

Q: What stands out to you about this passage?

Q: What does Jesus look for from us? (Deeds)

Q: Why are deeds important? (Reflect our heart)

Q: What was their issue? (Lukewarm)

Q: What did Jesus want them to be? (Hot or cold)

Q: Initially, when you read this passage, what does it mean to be hot and cold?

Q: What do you base that on?

Laodicea sat between two cities (Colossae and Hierapolis)

"Hot" means "boiling," referring to the hot springs of Hierapolis that brought physical healing to people who had arthritis at the time.

"Cold" refers to the cold springs of Colossae. Coldwater is refreshing and brought refreshment to the weary. (ref. **Isa. 55**) Cold is a good thing to be since Jesus wants us to be hot or cold. Jesus would not want anyone lost!

Q: What does it mean to be "lukewarm?"

The Roman Aqueduct system had allowed the two flows of water from both Hierapolis and Colossae to mix, meeting in Laodicea after having gathered all the minerals. The poor of Laodicea would drink this lukewarm water and making them sick. The cold water, when drunk from Colossae, was refreshing to the people. The hot water from Hierapolis brought warmth to the bones (from the hot water springs).

Jesus was saying the church was not bringing the refreshingly cold water of the gospel or the healing warm water of the gospel to a lost world. Therefore, Jesus wishes the church were cold or hot. Being Lukewarm made Jesus want to vomit (literally in the Greek).

Does your sin make you sick? Do you have the attitude of Jesus about mediocrity in the church?

Two options: Hot/Cold or Lukewarm.

Q: Were they in touch with their state of spirituality? (No)

Q: What did they think of themselves? v.17a (Struggled with being a rich city, the center of cosmetics at the time)

Q: What did Jesus think? v.17b

Q: What is scary about this?

Q: Can we know if we are lukewarm? (No)

Q: Can a church know? (No)

We need others in our lives because our sin blinds us. We need others to help us spiritually.

Q: According to this, when asked at the beginning of this study how your relationship with God is going—is it possible you did not have an accurate view?

Q: How does Jesus treat those He loves? (Rebukes and disciplines them.)

Jesus has left the building and is not in our hearts if we are lukewarm! (In context—He left the church!)

He is knocking at the door for you to let Him back in before it is too late!

Q: What prescription does Jesus give for sickness? (Repent, allow Jesus into your life and people into your life who are following Jesus)

Q: Why does Jesus say we must be earnest? (Life or death situation! There are Heaven and Hell! Where will you spend eternity if you were to die tonight?)

CHALLENGE: Are you hot/cold, or are you lukewarm? Maybe you have no relationship with Christ, so you are dead spiritually and need to be made alive in Christ! Be eager and repent! Get someone in your life who will love you like Jesus! You do not know where you are at spiritually. No one can answer the first question we asked.

JEHOIAKIM

*Variations of this Bible Talk have been done throughout the recent history of discipling ministries.

Assign: **Jeremiah 36 (v. 1-3; 4-6)** Explain.

Summarize **v. 7-19**

READ: **v. 20-26**

Activity: You will play the role of Jehoiakim and take out the unwanted parts of the Bible. Choose two scriptures to "cut them out." Maybe things that people have a hard time accepting or which an individual has a hard time obeying—the "undesirable" parts. Pair up guests with the person who brought them to help them in this activity. (The selected portions of Scripture are usually about sin, hell, the narrow road, etc.)

BREAK for a few minutes to do the above activity.

Go around and have each person explain what Scripture would be taken out and why it is being removed.

The leader brings the new version of Christianity to life by coming up with a name of the religion with the group and paints a picture of what it would look like to be part of a church that did not practice the deleted portions of Scripture.

Q: Would this be a pleasant "church" to be a part of? Why or why not?

Q: What does this teach us about God's commands?

Jeremiah 36:27-28; 31-32

Q: Did ignoring God's Word make it go away?

Q: What is the consequence?

Q: Do we have the right to play games with God's Word?

Q: How do we do this today?

Q: What lessons can be learned?

> **CHALLENGE:** Ignoring the Bible does not make it go away or less true. Study the Bible.

References

Bible Gateway, "Tyrannus." https://www.biblegateway.com/resources/encyclopedia-of-the-bible/Tyrannus, July 6, 2022.

Bright, Bill. *How to Make Your Mark*. Arrowhead Springs, CA: Here's Life Publishers, 1983, as cited by R. Rowland. *Campus Ministries: A Historical Study of Churches of Christ Campus Ministries and Selected College Ministries from 1706 to 1990*. Fort Worth: Star Publications, 1991.

Dimitry, Jason. *COPS Company of Prophets: Church Builders Field Manual*. SOPI, 2022.

Encyclopedia.com, "Student Volunteer Movement." Accessed September 4, 2022. https://www.encyclopedia.com/religion/encyclopedias-almanacs-transcripts-and-maps/student-volunteer-movement.

Fee, G., & Stuart, D. *How to Read the Bible for All It's Worth*. Zondervan, 2003.

Harding, Ron. *The Untold Story: Chronicles of Modern Day Christianity*. SoldOut Press, 2020.

"Reflection—Prayer at Hampden-Sydney College." Hearts for the Lost, September 7, 2022. https://heartsforthelost.com/posts/biblical-revival-a-historical-reflection-prayer-at-hampden-sydney-college/.

Love, William. "Folsom: A Perfect Place for Kids?" *East Bay Times,* September 29, 2005. **www.eastbaytimes.com/2005/09/29/folsom-a-perfect-place-for-kids.**

McSpadden, Kevin. "You Now Have a Shorter Attention Span than a Goldfish," *Time,* May 14, 2015. **https://time.com/3858309/attention-spans-goldfish/.**

Patterson, Mike. "How to Put a Sermon Together." Mike Patterson, 2013. YouTube Video, 1:7:27. **https://youtu.be/SkhkEuRMVSw.**

Rowland, R. *Campus Ministries: A Historical Study of Churches of Christ Campus Ministries and Selected College Ministries from 1706 to 1990.* Fort Worth, TX: Star Publications, 1991.

Smith, Casey. "Is this the Golden Age of College Student Activism?" *USA Today College,* March 23rd, 2017.

Spurgeon, Charles. "Tearful Sowing and Joyful Reaping," *Metropolitan Tabernacle Pulpit* Volume 15, April 25, 1869.

USD21.org. "SoldOut Discipling Movement." Accessed September 4, 2022. **https://usd21.org.**

Wilson, John F. "Campus Ministry Perspective on the World." Lecture, National Campus Ministers' Seminar, Search, AR, August 8, 1978.

Wilson, John F. "History of Campus Ministries in the Churches of Christ." Lecture for Religion 592 class, Campus Ministry Organizational and Administration, Pepperdine University, Malibu, CA, fall 1983.

Made in the USA
Middletown, DE
26 October 2022